TABLE OF CONTENTS

ABOUT THE STUDY

The intent of this study is to provide participants with a high level overview of the Bible, by tracing the key historical events, themes, and what role they play in redemptive history.

Our prayer for you is that His story becomes alive in your heart.

Each week the study has 3 components:

1. Scripture reading & questions (Some questions are marked,"★ **For a Deeper Dive.**" These are meant to highlight events and promises of God which will be fulfilled as HIStory unfolds.)

2. Summary reading – A brief commentary on where we are in HIStory (Summaries are all excerpts from HIStory in 30 Days: Genesis to Revelation with Daily Devotionals, Carole O. Schryber, WestBow Press, 2017)

3. Personal application questions

ABOUT THE AUTHORS

Carole O. Schryber

Carole Schryber is a wife and mother of three grown children. She was an attorney in New York who gave up the practice of law to devote herself to studying and teaching Scripture. She has used her research and analytical skills from the study of law for inductive Bible study.

For the past fifteen years she has been a Christian teacher, speaker and writer. Her talk, Genesis to Revelation in 60 Minutes, was the impetus for a devotional book she authored, HIStory in 30 Days: Genesis to Revelation. In addition to speaking and teaching at her home church of McLean Bible and other area churches, she was the former Associate Teaching Director of Community Bible Study in McLean, Virginia, which serves more than four hundred women weekly.

Natalie Walkley

Natalie Walkley is a wife, mother, and lover of good stories. She works full time in marketing, helping brands tell their story effectively to drive top-line growth. Natalie fell in love with God's Word through the inductive Bible study approach and realizing that the "ah-ha" moments with Scripture are not reserved just for pastors and theologians.

After starting her career in a year-long ministry development program at McLean Bible Church she has since been writing and leading Bible studies for the past decade. She currently leads a women's group study at her home church, The Village Chapel, where she focuses on inspiring a passion for Scripture, and empowering others to garner God's timeless truths for themselves through inductive study. Natalie and her husband, Matt, live in Nashville, Tennessee with their daughter.

WEEK 1:
In The Beginning

Scripture: Read Genesis 1–2 in its entirety.

1. When did God create the heavens and the earth? What does this timing tell you about the existence of God?

2. Note that God does not argue for His own existence in the Bible. HIStory presumes He was the creator and author of all. What are some reasons that you believe this statement to be true? Read Romans 1:20–21 for additional insight.

3. ★ **For a Deeper Dive:** As HIStory unfolds, you will discover that there is a triune (consisting of three in one) nature to God. How do you see the triune nature of God also in John 1:1–5 and Genesis 1:26?

4. Describe the order of creation in Genesis 1.

    How was each element created? What does this methodology tell you about God's power?

    What did God notice after each of His creations?

5. What was God's intent for creation? (For additional insight read Psalm 19:1; Psalm 136:1–9; John 1:3; Colossians 1:16; Romans 1:20)

6. Read Genesis 1:26-31 and Genesis 2:5-9. How was man created? How did this differ from the rest of creation?

[Author's Note: Genesis 1 is the "macro" account of the creation of all mankind, while Genesis 2 is the "micro" version of the creation of both male and female individually.]

7. What purposes did God give man in Genesis?

Read Revelation 4:11. What is God's ultimate purpose for man?

8. Read Genesis 2:18-25. Why did God create woman?

9. What do you think the word "helper" means?

Read Psalm 30:10. Who else in Scripture is referred to as a helper? How does this affect your perception of what a helper is?

(For additional occurrences of "helper" in Scripture see Deuteronomy 33:26, 29; Psalm 20:1-2; Psalm 121:1-2; John 14:26.)

10. How do you think God intended woman to be a "helper" to man?

11. How did God form the woman? How does this compare to how He formed man?

12. Read Genesis 1:27 again. Man and woman were created in the image of God. How did the first man and woman reflect the image (or the attributes) of God?

   In what ways are God's attributes distinct from mankind?

13. Imagine life in Eden after creation. What parts of Eden are appealing to you?

SUMMARY WEEK 1

HIStory begins...

"In the beginning, God..." Before there was anything—there was God. And not just God, but one God in three forms. GENESIS records that man was created in our image. There is a plurality to God—Father, Son, and Holy Spirit, which will be further revealed as the story unfolds.

In the beginning, God created. Out of nothing, He created, and He created by speaking. From God's mouth came all of creation. He created the heavens and the earth. He created light. He created the sky, stars, oceans, land, and vegetation. He created animals, including the creatures of the sea, birds of the air, and creatures of the land.

And after everything, God saw that it was good. Everything God created was good. There was nothing bad and nothing evil. And all of this came about because God spoke.

But God had more to do. He wanted something to demonstrate and witness His glory, provide fellowship, and rule over the rest of creation. To do all this, He created man. He wanted man to be in His image, though not necessarily physically. God would manifest Himself in different forms in Scripture through His attributes: the ability to communicate, think, reason, act, and love. While there was only one God—creator, omnipotent, and sovereign—man was created to share His attributes.

And man was distinguished from the rest of creation. He was not created from nothing, but from the dust of the ground. God Himself breathed into man's nostrils the breath of life, and man became a living being who would soon be called Adam.

God is good, and He didn't want Adam to be alone. Adam would need a helper. He'd need someone to come alongside of him to rule over the rest of creation. He'd need someone with strength and discernment. God paraded before Adam all the animals to name, but from these animals, no suitable helper was found. So from the rib of Adam, God created a woman who would soon be called Eve. She would be bone of his bones and flesh of his flesh. She'd be his helper. She'd live with Adam in this Eden. And while they couldn't create something from nothing, they were given the means to procreate.

God was pleased—it was indeed very good. God wanted man and woman to live for eternity with Him, without shame or guilt and without evil. And though they were naked, they felt no shame.

Personal Application

Consider the "power" it would require to be the Creator of all things. How does insight into this power impact your view of God?

Ut commodo facilisis nibh sed ipsum. Nunc semper magna vel consequat.

God not only created the Earth, but He also created the "order" to sustain life (i.e. gravity, systems, plants giving off oxygen, etc.) How does this fact expand your knowledge of God as a life-giver?

What implications (if any) are there for "created" beings?

The Hebrew word for "image" is tselem (tseh'-lem), which means "likeness of resemblance." Have you ever had someone tell you that you remind them of someone they know? How then might you look at that person more closely to see how you are similar or different?

Scripture says that mankind is made in the image of God. How might you look at God more carefully to better understand how/why you reflect His image?

If all people are made in His image, how do you think God values mankind versus the rest of creation?

List all of the things you have you learned from the creation story.

About God:

About man and woman:

Additional Notes:

WEEK 2:
Original Sin

Scripture: Read Genesis 2:15-17; 3:1-7

1. What was the command that God gave to man in the garden?

   Why do you think God gave this command?

2. What was the consequence for disobeying the command in the garden?

   As HIStory continues, the meaning of this consequence will be made clear, but other than physical death, what kind of death is referenced in Scripture? See Ephesians 2:1 for insight.

3. Reread Genesis 1:26-30. How would you have felt about this rule?

4. Who was the serpent, and what do you learn about him in Genesis 3:1?

5. Read Isaiah 14:12-14 and Ezekiel 28:12-15. What was Satan's sin that led him to stray from God's original intent?

6. What other names were given to the serpent in Scripture?

SCRIPTURE	NAME OF SATAN
Matthew 13:19, 38	
Matthew 12:24	
Luke 10:18	
John 12:31	
2 Corinthians 4:4	
2 Corinthians 11:14	
Ephesians 2:2	
1 Thessalonians 3:5	
Revelation 12:10	

7. Consider the following verbs used to describe Satan's actions:

SCRIPTURE	SATAN'S ACTIONS
Matthew 13:4, 19	
Matthew 13:25, 28	
John 10:12	
1 Peter 5:8	
Revelation 12:9	

8. What did the serpent ask the woman? How did he expand God's restriction?

9. What was the woman's response?

    Did she accurately articulate God's command?

10. How did the serpent deceive the woman? In other words, how did He entice her?

11. Define "sin" in your own words.

12. Do you think that God is the ultimate moral authority for man and woman? Why or why not?

13. How was it in the interest of the man and woman to obey God?

14. Considering the meaning of the word "helper" as defined in last week's lesson, how did the woman fail to fulfill God's purpose for her?

15. What happened to the man and woman after eating the fruit?

    Why did they cover themselves?

16. How would you define shame?

17. How does Satan still deceive people today? What methods does he use? Read John 10:10 for additional insight.

SUMMARY WEEK 2

HIStory continues...

Adam and Eve lived in ideal conditions in the Garden of Eden where their every need was fully met. God's will for them was to live in paradise with Him forever. As God walked and conversed with them, He had one command: "...You may surely eat of every tree of the garden, but of the tree of the knowledge of good and evil you shall not eat, for in the day that you eat of it you shall surely die" (Genesis 2:16–17). This was the first of several covenants God gave to man. It was conditional. Follow Me and you will live; reject Me and you will die. Adam and Eve had a part to play in this covenant. God asked for obedience, but He gave Adam and Eve the ability to choose obedience.

Why did God allow Adam and Eve to choose whether or not to be obedient? Because choosing obedience to God would demonstrate "relationship" and demonstrate that Adam and Eve trusted God even as to things they didn't understand. Disobedience to God would give them knowledge of what is outside God's will, and what is outside the will of God is evil. God wanted Adam and Eve to be holy, as He is holy.

Adam and Eve weren't alone in the Garden. Satan, in the form of a serpent, was there. God didn't create Satan as evil. God created him as a good angel in the heavens who could follow God's will. But Satan had chosen separation from God. There in Eden, Satan wanted to tempt Adam and Eve to disobey God and thereby gain the knowledge of evil. Satan lied and tricked the woman. He misquoted God's command. Even though God hadn't given Adam and Eve a reason not to trust Him, Satan's intention was for man and woman to doubt God's goodness and to make them believe that God was withholding something from them. Satan tempted them into believing that if they ate of the tree of the knowledge of good and evil, they would be "like God." They would have the same wisdom as God, so they wouldn't need God. The trust relationship would be broken. Satan tempted them, saying: "...You will not surely die. For God knows that when you eat of it your eyes will be opened, and you will be like God, knowing good and evil" (Genesis 3:4–5).

"Oh, to be like God," Eve perhaps thought! It wasn't good enough to believe God and trust Him when He said there was something called evil. Eve disobeyed. She questioned God—the same loving God who'd given them everything in the Garden of Eden. God's perfect will for man and woman was that they'd never disobey. But God's permissive will was to give them the choice of obedience and life. The story of Adam and Eve demonstrated that even with the abundance in paradise, man and woman chose not to obey God.

Adam and Eve ate the fruit. Sin is the choice to know evil or that which is against God's perfect and holy will. The source of their sin was pride. They felt they deserved more. In the moment they disobeyed, guilt flooded into them for the first time, and it separated them from God. The perfect image of God was scarred. Adam and Eve hid from God. Much as disobedient children might hide from their parents in shame, Adam and Eve covered their naked bodies in shame. Yet their covering, fig leaves, was inadequate to make atonement for their disobedience.

Personal Application

Do you think it is fair that God had a rule in the garden? Why or why not?

It's easy to look at Adam & Eve and think that we would have acted differently. Do you feel that you could have resisted the deception of the serpent? Why or why not?

While we are no longer in the garden of Eden like Eve and Adam, how are we similarly tempted in the same way? Read 1 John 2:16 for additional insight.

How does this week's lesson help you know the enemy and his tactics?

What did you learn about yourself and your tendencies?

When Adam & Eve were confronted with their sin, they hid in shame. Can you think of a time that you felt shame?

What are the things that people do to "cover up" their shame?

[Author's Note: People often use the words guilt and shame interchangeably. However, the distinction is important. Guilt is the recognition that we have violated a moral standard or a law. Shame, on the other hand, reflects how we feel about our guilt. Thankfully, HIStory will reveal that God removes both our guilt and our shame. It is part of the story of redemption revealed to mankind!]

Additional Notes:

WEEK 3:
Separation from God

"By faith Abel offered to God a more acceptable sacrifice than Cain, through which he was commended as righteous, God commending him by accepting His gifts. And through His faith, though he died, he still speaks."

—HEBREWS 11:4

Scripture: Read Genesis 3:8-24; Genesis 4

1. Define "curse" in your own words.

2. What was the first part of the curse that God gave to the serpent in Genesis 3:14?

3. Consider Genesis 3:15a, "I will put enmity between you and the woman, and between your offspring and her offspring."

    a. What does "enmity" mean? (Use a dictionary if necessary.)

    b. Who is the offspring/seed of the woman referring to?

    c. ⭐ **For a Deeper Dive:** Do you see enmity in the world today between Satan (and his offspring) and the offspring of the woman?

[Author's Note: The Bible not only identifies the enmity between Satan and the woman (and their respective offspring), but the enmity that is created with ourselves and God when we sin. "Do you not know that friendship with the world is enmity with God? Therefore whoever wishes to be a friend of the world makes himself an enemy of God" (James 4:4). "Do not love the world or the things in the world. If anyone loves the world, the love of the Father is not in him" (1 John 2:15).]

4. Who do you think is the "he" in "he shall bruise your head?" See Genesis 3:15.

Given that the head is a vital part of the body, what does this tell you?

[Author's Note: the word for "bruise" (shuwph in Hebrew) means to break or to crush, implying that this would be a fatal blow.]

★ **For a Deeper Dive:** How is this a promise of future hope for man and woman?

5. Who is the "you" in "you shall bruise his heel"? What does this statement imply?

Given that a heel is a non-vital part of the body, what does this fact tell you?

6. Describe the curse to the woman. How do you see the effects of this today?

7. Describe the curse to man. How do you see the effects of this today?

8. What is the first thing God did for Adam and Eve after explaining the consequences for their sin?

   Why is His action significant? Read Genesis 3:21.

9. After Adam and Eve sinned, how did they become like God? How was this different from their original image?

10. God said in Genesis 2:16, "You may surely eat of every tree of the garden, but of the tree of the knowledge of good and evil you shall not eat, for in the day that you eat of it you shall surely die." Read Genesis 3:23-24. How do we see the physical and spiritual consequences of sin? (For additional insight see James 1:15.)

    How is this separation the "death" of something?

11. Read Genesis 4:1-16. What were the offerings that Cain and Abel brought to the Lord?

12. Why did God have regard for Abel and his offering, but for Cain and his offering he had no regard? Consider Hebrews 11:4. How did Abel's view of God differ from Cain's?

13. How would you define faith?

14. What parallels do you see between the story of Adam/Eve and Cain/Abel? (Hint: look specifically at what God says in His interaction with them.)

15. List all of the things you learn about sin from the account of Cain and Abel.

16. The New Testament book of Jude (verse 11) refers to "the way of Cain." What does this phrase mean?

    Likewise, what does 1 John 3:12 say about Cain? How does this verse shed more light into Cain's heart?

17. What were the ultimate consequences of Cain's sin?

18. How do we still see God's graciousness to both Adam, Eve, and Cain?

SUMMARY WEEK 3

HIStory continues...

Like a good and loving parent would know, there had to be punishment for sin and consequences for disobeying God. Love requires justice. Yet before God enumerated the consequences, He demonstrated grace to humankind. He cursed Satan: "...on your belly you shall go, and dust you shall eat all the days of your life. I will pust enmity between you and the woman, and between your offspring and her offspring" (Genesis 3:14b-15a).

The dictionary defines "enmity" as a feeling or condition of hostility or hatred. God promised that hatred would arise between the serpent and the woman. Satan would be allowed to exist in the world as a despised creature, and he'd tempt the descendants of woman. There would always be a battle between them—for goodness and evil can never reconcile. Had God stopped there, the future would have been discouraging and hopeless for man and woman. But God continued with a promise of destruction to the serpent.

God gave just a glimmer of His grace and plan to rid the world of evil and destroy Satan. "...He shall bruise your head, and you shall bruise his heel" (Genesis 3:15). The promise seems vague, but it will be further explained as the story unfolds. Essentially, it was a promise of a Savior. Who would this "he" be? This is the first reference to a hero of the story. The "he" would be an offspring of Eve who would bruise the head of the offspring of the serpent (Satan). The word "bruise" is rendered from the Hebrew word "crush," which means to break into pieces or greatly injure. The head is a vital organ and, when crushed, is fatal. Satan would be destroyed. The Savior would have his "heel bruised." A bruise to the heel isn't fatal. The Savior would live.

There would come a time when the enmity would no longer exist. God, through our "bruised" Savior, would deem us to be without knowledge of evil. Relationship with God would be restored. While we're not told the specifics in Genesis of how this would happen or which offspring of Eve would be the Savior, God told us there would be a happy ending. God had set in motion a plan of hope, the promise of a Savior—a hero unlike any other.

God then enumerated the consequences to Adam and Eve for their sin. Eve now had pain in childbirth and Adam had to toil hard. Adam and Eve couldn't eat from the tree of life and live forever. They'd both suffer and ultimately experience a physical death and return to dust. Man and woman now knew evil by the pain of experiencing it. The loving God had wanted them to be spared that pain by trusting Him, but Adam and Eve chose disobedience. Finally, until their physical deaths, they'd experience a spiritual death—a separation from God. No longer would God walk with them in the garden. They were banished from the Garden of Eden. From that moment on, all humans had sin born into them. The children of Adam and Eve and all their descendants were no longer reflections of the image of God—love, joy, and goodness in its purest form. That image was scarred, and Adam and Eve would bear children in their own sinful image.

God's punishment didn't cause this spiritual death. The spiritual death was a result of sin and sin itself creates a separation from God. Adam and Eve demonstrated this by their desire to cover their naked bodies out of guilt and shame. But God is loving and gracious, and from the beginning, He provided a means for temporary reconciliation with Him.

An animal was killed, and God Himself made garments of skin for Adam and Eve to cover their nakedness and shame. God provided the means of atonement. God established that an innocent animal would have to die as a substitute to atone for the sin of man and woman. It would be the blood from that animal that would reconcile man with God. Killing an innocent animal wasn't a cruel act of God. Life is in the blood, and the visual of seeing the blood was to show man and woman that their selfish act was so serious as to cause death. The death of the animal was meant to teach them about the cost of sin.

The scarred image of God was evident through Eve's first offspring. She gave birth to Cain and Abel. Abel's sacrifice, made with faith, was the blood of a firstborn innocent animal. This was pleasing to God. Cain's sacrifice, made without faith, was the fruit of the land. This was not pleasing to God. Cain was jealous that God favored Abel's sacrifice. The first murder was committed when Cain killed Abel. Sin breeds more sin.

Personal Application

Think about how Adam responded when God asked what he had done. Now think about how Eve responded. What do their responses have in common?

Think of one of the last times that you did something wrong. Did you blameshift at all? If so, what did you blame? A person? A circumstance? Something else? Explain.

What is the alternative to blaming others for our own sin?

How can you practice this more regularly?

What prevents you from seeing your sin for what it is?

Have you experienced "the way of Cain" in your own life? In other words, how have you seen your sin bring about death, destruction and grave consequences? Think of 1-2 specific examples and explain them below.

For Adam, Eve, and Cain their sin directly impacted their relationship with God. Isaiah 59:2 says, "but your iniquities have made a separation between you and your God, and your sins have hidden His face from you so that he does not hear." What sins in your life might be separating you from fellowship with God?

Additional Notes:

WEEK 4:
God Favors Noah

> *"...Noah was a righteous man, blameless in his generation. Noah walked with God."*

– GENESIS 6:9

Scripture: Read Genesis 4:17-26; Genesis 5–9

1. As a consequence for killing Abel, Cain was sent away from the presence of the Lord (Genesis 4:16), although his life was spared. Look at the lineage of Cain. How do you see the "way of Cain" continuing in the next generations? What does this tell you about the natural condition of mankind's heart?

2. Read Genesis 5:1-3. What do you notice about Adam's son, Seth? How was he different from the man that God first created?

   What does this indicate about the condition of man since the Fall described in Genesis 3?

3. While Cain's line became entirely evil, some from the line of Seth began to call upon the name of the Lord (Genesis 4:26; 5:22). From what lineage did Noah come?

   How did Noah differ from the rest of man during his generation? See Genesis 6:1-8.

4. What do you learn about man from Genesis 6:5-8?

What do you learn about God?

5. Why do you think that the sin of man grieves God?

What three things about Noah do you learn in Genesis 6:9? See also 2 Peter 2:5. Define these attributes.

6. What does the phrase "But Noah found favor in the eyes of the Lord" imply about the reason Noah was chosen?

The word for "favor" in the Hebrew language can also be translated as "grace." How does this insight impact your understanding of why Noah was chosen?

7. What did God determine to do as the result of the earth's corruption?

8. Define the word "flesh" as used in Genesis 6:12. Also read Romans 8:1-8.

What does it mean to act according to the flesh? (Note: Some translations don't use the word "flesh." To see it clearly, read the passages in ESV, NASB, or KJV translation.)

9. Describe the ark that God told Noah to build.

10. What were all the things that God told Noah to do?

What expression is repeated to demonstrate Noah's obedience?

11. Imagine being Noah—living in a generation of world-wide wickedness. Do you think it would have been easy to do "all that God has commanded you"?

12. Who did God spare from the flood?

What was only thing that Noah's family had to do to be saved?

13. What was the first thing that Noah did after coming out from the ark? See Genesis 8:20–22.

[Author's Note: As we saw with Cain and Abel, offerings were made as an act of worship, and were to be made with faith. Later in HIStory, God will further define the various types of offerings.]

★ **For a Deeper Dive:** What is a burnt offering? See Leviticus 1 for insight.

14. Read Genesis 9:1–7, what did God tell Noah to do after the ground dried up?

15. Read Genesis 9: 8–17 and define the word covenant. (Use a Bible dictionary or concordance if necessary.)

16. What was the covenant that God made with Noah?

Who did the covenant apply to?

(Note: We will see several different covenants God makes with His people. Be sure to pay special attention to them and keep note of who they are with.)

17. By saving Noah and his family, how did God preserve His promise regarding the offspring of Eve? See Genesis 3:14–15.

18. Identify all of the things you learned about God from this account of Noah and the flood.

SUMMARY WEEK 4

HIStory continues...

As man and woman multiplied, they became increasingly wicked: "The Lord saw that the wickedness of man was great in the earth, and that every intention of the thoughts of his heart was only evil continually" (Genesis 6:5). Humans had become so depraved. "And the Lord regretted that he had made man on the earth, and it grieved him to his heart" (Genesis 6:6). God chose to send rain to destroy those who sought the knowledge of evil. He would leave an indelible mark indicating that the wages of sin is death. It would have been easy for God to wipe out everyone and begin again, but God demonstrated that redemption was available for the righteous. It was another picture of God's grace.

One man, Noah, had found favor with God. Noah walked with God, not perfectly, he was sinful, but he sought to do the will of God. Noah was told to build an ark when it's possible that it had never rained. He obeyed and built the ark in the precise dimensions God commanded. Noah preached to the people, but they didn't heed his warning. God gave the people a veritable lifetime to turn to Him during the many years the ark was being built. Finally, the doors of the ark closed. It was too late to board, and the floods came. The time of God's mercy was over. Noah's family was in the lifesaving boat. The rest who didn't seek to follow God were outside of the boat. At any earlier time, the people could have entered. Like Adam and Eve, they heard the word of God and chose to reject it. This was also a foreshadowing of a future time, when it would be too late to receive God's salvation for eternity.

Because Noah's family was saved, at the end of the flood, they were given responsibility for governing the world for God. God had preserved a people. The promise of a "bruised" Savior from Eve's offspring was preserved. The Savior was still to come.

God gave a sign of His peace and grace—the dove. Noah made his sacrifice at the altar, and God promised that never again would He cover the earth with a flood. He marked this covenant with a rainbow.

But a cycle, begun with Adam and Eve, would be repeated over and over through history. Man and woman would sin, God would judge, blood would have to be shed to remind man and woman that their sin had consequences, God would forgive, then God would give a sign of hope. His grace would restore and redeem when the people couldn't rescue themselves. God would preserve those who walked with him.

Personal Application

How would you answer the question, "are people inherently good?" based on what you have read so far? Explain.

Describe the first time that you realized you were capable of sin.

Is blameless the same thing as sinless? Why or why not?

A lot of people struggle with the idea of God wiping out the Earth. How do you reconcile the flood with God's goodness? (For more insight read Psalm 86:15; 1 Peter 3:20.)

What do you think it would say about God if He was passive about the evilness of mankind? Would you want to live in a world where sin was given full reign?

What makes it difficult at times to do all that the Lord commands?

Despite our sinfulness, how can we walk with God as Noah did? What does walking with God look like practically?

How does the historical account of Noah demonstrate God's grace to mankind?

Additional Notes:

WEEK 5:
Abraham is Chosen

"And he [Abraham] believed the Lord, and he counted it to him as righteousness."

GENESIS 15:6

(Note: this week has quite a bit more Scripture to read through. To make it easier to follow, we have broken up the questions with the passages relevant to them. However you may want to block off a bit more time to complete this week's study.)

Scripture: Read Genesis 11:27–13:18

1. Where did Abram's journey begin? Where did God direct him to go? (For additional insight see Act 7:2-3.)

   What does the journey tell you about how Abram first trusted God?

2. Genesis 12:1-3, 12:7-8, 13:14-18, 15:7-18 contain what is known as the Abrahamic Covenant. Describe the 3 three major parts of the covenant in the chart below.

COVENANT PROMISE	DETAILS
Land	
People	
Blessing	

[Author's Note: The Abrahamic covenant is known as a unilateral covenant. Generally, when two parties were forming a covenant, they would pass through the two parts of the animal sacrifice to seal the agreement. However, Genesis 15 describes how God alone passed through and sealed the covenant showing that He would be the one to fulfill it; the promise was not contingent on Abram's obedience.]

★ **For a Deeper Dive:** Who is the "blessing" foreshadowing? See Galatians 3:14.

3. Why would this covenant have been personally pleasing to Abram? (Consider the size of his family at the time. See Genesis 11:30.)

4. Referring to Genesis 11:27–12:10, describe Abram's journey. Where did they travel?

    What did Abram do to honor God along the journey?

5. The Promised Land had no large rivers or source for water. Anyone living in this area would have to be dependant on rain and God's provisions. Read the account of Abram in Genesis 12:10–20. What does this passage tell you about Abram's early walk of faith?

    Do you think it was God's desire for Abram to go to Egypt? List all the things that Abram could have learned about God during this time of his life.

Scripture: Read Genesis 17; Genesis 21:1-7.

6. Read Genesis 17:15-19. What did God clarify to Abram about the promised heir?

7. Genesis 15:6 says that Abram "believed the Lord, and He counted it to him as righteousness." Practically speaking, what is the difference between believing there is a god and believing God?

8. What did God require of Abram as a "sign" of the covenant? Read Genesis 17:9-14.

   Define the word "sign" using a concordance.

   What is the difference between a condition of a covenant and a sign of a covenant?

9. Abram (who God renamed Abraham) and Sarai (who God renamed Sarah) had to wait many years for the birth of their son; Abram was 75 when the covenant was made, and 100 when their son, Isaac was born. What does this waiting period tell us about God and God's timeline?

Scripture: Read Genesis 22.

10. What was the test that God gave to Abraham?

11. How did Abraham demonstrate his faith in the Lord?

12. What did God say was the reason "to not lay a hand on the boy"?

13. How did God demonstrate His faithfulness?

14. What have you learned so far about the Lord's requirement of a blood sacrifice for the atonement of sin? Describe the occurrences where you have seen it up to this point in Scripture.

HISTORICAL ACCOUNT	SCRIPTURE	DESCRIPTION
Adam & Eve	Gen 3:21	
Noah	Gen 8:20	

15. By preserving the life of Isaac, how was the promise in Genesis 3:15 preserved?

16. God reaffirmed His covenant in Genesis 22:17-18. What do you know so far about God's plan to redeem the world? See Galatians 3:16.

SUMMARY WEEK 5

HIStory continues...

During the many years that followed, the population grew. God hadn't forgotten His promise that one from the offspring of Eve would destroy Satan. How would this one be identified? There were, after all, a lot of people born from Eve's lineage. God would want this Savior to be recognized. So God selected one man, Abraham, from Eve's lineage. It would be through Abraham that we could trace the offspring going forward.

He was a man with nothing, and yet it would be through him that God would expand the promise to send a Savior. Abraham was a nomad living in the land of Ur when God called him to leave his homeland and travel to a place that God would show him. Abraham obeyed, and God made a covenant with Abraham that had several components:

1. A promise of a **people**: Abraham would be the father of a great nation.

2. A promise of a **land**: Abraham was promised the land upon which Abraham was standing—the Promised Land. It would belong one day to His, to God's, chosen people. (God planned this as a foreshadowing of a future place for God's people.)

3. A promise of a **blessing**: Through Abraham the nations of the earth would be blessed.

This was a unique covenant. Only one party was necessary. It had no conditions. It wasn't dependent on anything Abraham or his descendants did or did not do. Unlike the covenant that God had made with Adam that had the condition "do not eat," God alone would keep this covenant with Abraham. This would be part of the plot, and the fulfillment of the covenant would unfold in the pages of the Bible.

God made this covenant not because Abraham and his offspring were better than anyone else or more deserving. As stated previously, Abraham and his offspring were chosen so we could identify the promised Savior when He came. Abraham's family would also be witnesses who could testify and record all that God did. This would provide the evidence to link the Savior with the promise of the covenant. To the world, it would seem like an impossible promise to keep. Abraham and his wife, Sarah, were very old when God made this promise. How would Abraham have descendants as numerous as the stars? This made no more sense to Abraham than God's statement to Noah to build an ark.

While Abraham had moments of impatience—for God made him wait—he believed. And finally, Sarah had a miracle baby in her old age. Witnesses would have to think: "It must have been God" to give a baby when it was scientifically impossible. The Bible records many instances where God performs a miracle so that the people will know that He is God. This miracle would also foreshadow the birth of the future Savior, whose birth would also be scientifically impossible.

Abraham continued to walk with God in obedience. Yet as righteous as Abraham was, he wasn't without sin. Sin separates us from a holy God. To atone for sin, a sacrifice had to be made to God. On one occasion, God tested Abraham's obedience. He asked Abraham to offer up his son, Isaac, as a sacrifice. Abraham trusted God. He knew God would somehow keep His promise of numerous descendants, and therefore, in faith, Abraham brought Isaac to the altar. Abraham told Isaac that God would provide a lamb for the sacrifice. Abraham and God were so close, and yet how painful it must have been for Abraham to walk up the mountain, prepared to sacrifice his beloved son Isaac.

Just as Abraham was about to strike Isaac, an angel stopped him. A ram—caught in thorns—was in the thicket. The ram took the place of Isaac and became the blood sacrifice to cover Abraham's sin. Abraham called this place, "the Lord will provide." Certainly, Abraham knew the Lord had and would always keep His promises.

Personal Application

What is the opposite of trust?

There are several instances that demonstrate that Abraham had faith (or trusted) God. Do you trust God to provide for you? In what areas of your life have you trusted him before? How has God proven Himself trustworthy?

In what areas of your life (or circumstances) do you have a difficult time trusting God? Explain why.

Is it possible to cultivate trust in God? If so, how can we practically cultivate the kind of trust in God (faith) that Abraham had? List some ways below.

God asked Abraham to give up his most cherished thing—his own son. Sometimes God asks us to "give up" things (even good things!) so we can trust Him more fully. These things can be potential idols, or good things that simply mean too much to us. What "Isaac" do you potentially have in your life that God may be asking you to lay down? Jot down your thoughts.

Additional Notes:

WEEK 6:
Joseph Shows Forgiveness

"But Joseph said to them, 'Do not fear, for am I in the place of God? As for you, you meant evil against me, but God meant it for good, to bring it about that many people should be kept alive, as they are today. So do not fear; I will provide for you and your little ones.' Thus he comforted them and spoke kindly to them."

– GENESIS 50:19-21

1. Part of the Promise to Abraham was that through an offspring the nations of the world would be blessed. Trace the descendants of Abraham through the following Scripture.

    Use Genesis 25:19-27 and 35:9-12; 22-26 to fill out the chart below.

Abraham's Genealogy

Abraham	Sarah

	Rebekah

twins

The two nations ——→ | Esau |

The 12 tribes ——→ | 12 Sons |

Scripture: Genesis 37–50

(Note: This is a long section of Scripture. Rather than reading through it for every detail, read it through as you would the chapters of a novel to glean the overall plot and story of Joseph.)

1. Trace Joseph's life, recording the significant events. (Note: Anytime someone wrongs Joseph or he is treated unfairly, mark that event with an asterisk or a special symbol.)

    a. Genesis 37:1-11 (Specifically, what do you learn about the relationship between Joseph and his father, and Joseph and his brothers?)

    b. Genesis 37:12-36

    c. Genesis 39

    d. Genesis 40–41:36

    e. Genesis 41:37-56

    f. Genesis 42

    g.   Genesis 43

    h.   Genesis 44

    i.   Genesis 45

    j.   Genesis 46:1-7

    k.   Genesis 47:1-12, 27-30

2.   List all the times Joseph was wronged or treated unfairly, and the people involved.

3.   What emotions does Joseph experience during all these unfair/wrong circumstances?

4.   Read again Genesis 45:4-15 and 50:19-21. Despite everything Joseph had been through (and how they had treated him) how does Joseph treat his brothers?

5.   What do you learn about Joseph's character through this portion of Scripture?

6.   What can we learn about forgiveness from Joseph?

7.   Three times in Chapter 39 it is recorded, "The Lord was with Joseph." While Joseph's life was filled with much adversity, how do you see the truth of this statement?

8.   How was the promise to Abraham preserved?

[Author's Note: In Genesis 50:20, Joseph says to his brothers, "As for you, you meant evil against me, but God meant it for good, to bring it about that many people should be kept alive, as they are today." While this verse is specific to Joseph's family, it also illustrates the continuation of God's blessing to Abraham. Joseph's position enabled him to preserve his family despite a famine, and thus preserving the lineage of the Promised Savior.]

9.   Genesis 49:8–10 records Jacob's prophecy regarding each of his sons. Record the prophecy regarding Judah. What does this tell us about the future lineage of the promised Savior?

10. ★ **For a Deeper Dive:** Joseph is often considered a "type" of Christ. (A type is a foreshadowing or prefiguring of the Savior.) What do you learn about the character of the promised Savior (offspring of Abraham) and His promised mission, from the story of Joseph?

11. Read Genesis 50:22–26. Where were God's people when Genesis ends? What did Joseph foresee for their future?

How did this demonstrate his trust in God's promises?

SUMMARY WEEK 6

HIStory continues...

Abraham knew that God would keep His promise of blessing the world through Abraham's descendant. The promise to bless was somehow tied to a blood sacrifice that God would provide. One day, an innocent intervener, wearing His own crown of thorns, would emerge as the sacrifice to atone for all the sins of man once and for all. Because the promised descendant and Savior would need to be recognized, the lineage of Abraham had to be carefully recorded.

Abraham's son Isaac had two sons, Esau and Jacob. While the two were still in the womb of Rebekah, Isaac's wife, they struggled with each other. The Lord told Rebekah that these twins would grow into two nations that would always be divided. God also told Rebekah that the older twin would serve the younger. And just as God had foretold, when Isaac was dying, his younger son, Jacob, deceived his father into bequeathing the "blessing" to him rather than to the oldest son, Esau.

The blessing would be more than a material blessing. It would mean that God's promise to Abraham would pass through Jacob, the younger. It seemed incredible that the promise would be fulfilled through a deceitful man. Yet one night after Jacob wrestled with God, he subordinated his own will to God's. Afterward, God renamed him "Israel," which means one who "reigns with God." This was an illustration for future generations. When God's people have an encounter with Him, a transformation takes place. The descendants of Isaac's son Esau would be the Edomites. They would choose to battle with Israel for generations.

Jacob (Israel) had twelve sons who represented the twelve tribes of Israel. Joseph was the youngest son of Israel. His jealous older brothers resented the favor their father showed Joseph and plotted to get rid of him. They sold him into slavery in Egypt. Though Joseph endured many trials as a slave in Egypt, he remained true to God, praising Him for all things. Eventually, Joseph found himself before the pharaoh. The pharaoh found favor in Joseph—such that he appointed Joseph to a high position in the Egyptian government. Joseph was credited with saving Egypt from a famine. The famine also devastated Israel. But God's providence intervened to protect Abraham's descendants.

Because of Joseph's high position in Egypt, he was able to provide food to the brothers who had betrayed him. Without Joseph's grace, God's people would have perished, and God's promise wouldn't have been kept. God's people would always need saving. Joseph would also serve as a picture of the Savior to come, whose grace and mercy would be extended to sinful and undeserving people.

Personal Application

What has this week's lesson taught you about God's divine providence, or governance over all situations to accomplish His purposes?

God can use anything (even a series of unfortunate events) in our lives to work in and through us. In what ways have you seen God at work, maybe even behind the scenes, in some of the most difficult experiences in your life? Do you tend to recognize this truth in the moment, or in retrospect? Explain.

What emotions do you experience when someone wrongs you?

How does not forgiving those who have wronged us impact us negatively?

The importance of forgiveness is a theme throughout the Bible. Why do you think forgiving others matters to God?

In our lives, we are going to have people that hurt us. In fact, you probably already have someone who has hurt you. Maybe not as badly as Joseph, or maybe so. Think about someone that has wronged you that you have not forgiven. Is the Lord calling you to forgive them?

[Author's Note: It is worth noting that there is a difference between forgiveness (one sided) and reconciliation of a relationship (two-sided). Not every relationship is healthy/safe enough for reconciliation, but that doesn't negate the one-sided responsibility of forgiveness that God commands.]

Additional Notes:

WEEK 7:
Call of Moses

"When the Lord saw that he turned aside to see, God called to him out of the bush, "Moses, Moses?" And he said, "Here I am." Then he said, "Do not come near; take your sandals off your feet, for the place on which you are standing is holy ground." And he said, "I am the God of your father, the God of Abraham, the God of Isaac, and the God of Jacob."

– EXODUS 3:4-6

Scripture: Read Exodus 1–4

1. While God's people settled in Egypt, what happened to their numbers? How did this begin to fulfill God's promise to Abraham?

2. How were the Egyptians treating the Israelites when Exodus begins? How does this confirm what God had told Abraham in Genesis 15:13-14?

3. What was Pharaoh's command to the midwives? Did the midwives obey him?

4. What does it mean to fear God? See Proverbs 1:7; Deuteronomy 10:12, 20–21; Hebrews 12:28-29.

    How were the midwives blessed for fearing the Lord?

5. Recount in your own words the story of Moses in Exodus 2:1-10. How did God protect Moses?

6. Read Exodus 2:11-15 and Acts 7:23-29. Moses saw the injustice that the Egyptians were doing to one of his people, and acted impulsively to remedy the situation. How effective was Moses' own plan to rescue his people? What were the negative consequences for Moses?

7. Read Acts 7:30-34 together with Exodus 3:1-6. How many years was Moses in the wilderness of Midian? How did God identify Himself to Moses in Exodus 3? What do you think it means to be on "holy ground"?

8. What did God ask of Moses? Why?

9. Why do you think God "called" Moses 40 years after he had been a prince in Egypt?

10. What is the name that God gave Himself? Why is His name significant? See Exodus 3:13-14.

11. What other names does God use to describe himself? What do they tell you about God?

HEBREW NAME	SCRIPTURE	ENGLISH TRANSLATION	MEANING
Elohim	Gen 1:1		
Yahweh	Gen 2:4		
Adonai	Gen 15:2		
El Shaddai	Gen 49:24		
El Roi	Gen 16:13		

12. As you read Exodus 3:11- 4:17, list all of Moses' objections to God's call on his life. What was God's response to each of Moses' concerns?

SCRIPTURE	MOSES' OBJECTIONS / DOUBTS / FEARS	GOD'S RESPONSE
Ex 3:11		
Ex 4:1		
Ex 4:10		
Ex 4:13		

13. What caused the Lord's anger in Exodus 4:13-14?

Despite Moses' final doubt what was God's provision? What does this tell you about God?

14. ★ **For a Deeper Dive:** What do the the following verses tell you about God's ability and promises to equip you for His purposes?

    a. Hebrews 13:20

    b. Philippians 1:6

    c. 2 Corinthians 4:7

SUMMARY WEEK 7

HIStory continues...

God's people multiplied. (God's promise to Abraham of a people.) They resided, however, in Egypt. How would God keep His other promise? (God's promise to Abraham of a land.) Genesis ended with the death of Joseph in Egypt. Joseph was a man of faith. Before he died, he made his sons promise that one day his bones would be moved from Egypt to the Promised Land. He knew all God's promises to Abraham, including the one of land, would one day come to pass.

Genesis demonstrated that the people God created would sin. The enmity between Satan and the offspring of Eve would continue. Man and woman would choose not to follow God. And yet God had already set in motion a plan to redeem them and to reconcile His sinful people to Himself. (God's promise to Abraham of a blessing.)

The story continues in EXODUS. Within four hundred years after Joseph's death, the descendants of Abraham in Egypt were so numerous they were perceived as a threat to the dictatorial power of the existing pharaoh. The pharaoh responded by enslaving God's people. Despite this enslavement, the population continued to grow just as God had promised. The more they were oppressed, the more they multiplied. So the pharaoh came up with another plan. He instructed the midwives to kill the newborn boys of the Israelites. When the fear of the God of Israel prevented the midwives from carrying out the pharaoh's command, the pharaoh then ordered that every boy born to God's people be thrown into the Nile. This plan, if successful, would have extinguished the descendants of Israel. God's promise to bless the world with a Savior from the offspring of Eve and from a descendant of Abraham would have been thwarted.

God needed to rescue His people once again. For this purpose, He selected Moses. Though Moses was one of the newborns sentenced to death by the pharaoh, he was saved. His mother placed him in a basket that she floated down the Nile. It was the pharaoh's own daughter who retrieved the basket from the Nile, rescued Moses, and raised him as her own. Moses grew to become a proud leader in the Egyptian military before God revealed to him his true heritage. Moses was called to rescue the people of God.

At first, he attempted to rescue the Israelites without God's help. Moses was appalled to see one of his people being physically abused by an Egyptian. Impulsively, Moses intervened and killed the Egyptian. When the pharaoh heard this, he wanted Moses killed. Moses became a fugitive living in exile. Without God, he demonstrated he was powerless.

Forty years later, God appeared to Moses in the burning bush and again called him to rescue the Israelites out of Egypt. A humbled Moses declared: "...Who am I that I should go to Pharaoh and bring the children of Israel out of Egypt?" (Exodus 3:11). God's answer to Moses's doubt was to remind Moses that He, God, would be with Him. The people would be saved not through the strength of Moses, but through the work of God. God further declared: "... Say this to the people of Israel, I AM has sent me to you" (Exodus 3:14).

Personal Application

Exodus 2:24-25 says, "And God heard their groaning, and God remembered His covenant with Abraham, with Isaac, and with Jacob. God saw the people of Israel—and God knew." How does it comfort you that God hears, sees, remembers, and knows you and your situations?

How does reflecting on God's character (described through His names) change how you might live your day-to-day life?

Have you ever been called by God for a task or mission that you felt ill-equipped to carry out? If so, what was it? How did you respond? How are you responding now?

How have you seen God equip you?

Moses had several "objections" (or excuses) for why he didn't feel equipped for the task God was calling him to. What objections do you tend to hide behind when it comes to serving God more fully?

Moses was a great man of God, yet struggled by letting his insecurities, fears, and doubts dictate his response to God's call. How does the example of Moses encourage and exhort you to take action in certain areas of your life?

Additional Notes:

WEEK 8:
The Passover Lamb

"Say therefore to the people of Israel, 'I am the Lord, and I will bring you out from under the burdens of the Egyptians, and I will deliver you from slavery to them, and I will redeem you with an outstretched arm and with great acts of judgment. I will take you to be my people, and I will be your God, and you shall know that I am the Lord your God, who has brought you out from under the burdens of the Egyptians.'"

– EXODUS 6:6-7

Scripture: Select passages from Exodus 5–14

Read Exodus 5–6 (Let My People Go)

1. What was God's stated purpose for asking Pharaoh to release the Israelites? See Exodus 7:16. (For additional insight see Exodus 8:1; 9:1, 13; 10:3)

    What does this tell you about His purpose for our own lives?

2. What was Pharaoh's response to Moses' command, "Let my people go" as recorded in Exodus 5:2? How is knowledge of the Lord related to obedience to Him?

3. What was the consequence for the Israelites?

4. God's promise in Exodus 6:1-9 is a beautiful declaration of His plan for His people. List out below what God said He would do.

    What do you learn about the plan and about God from these verses?

Read Exodus 7–12 (The Plagues)

5. Skim Exodus 7–12 to complete the following chart on the plagues.

VERSE	PLAGUE	COULD THE MAGICIANS DO IT?	PHARAOH'S RESPONSE	UNIQUE ASPECTS
Ex 7:14–25	Nile turned to blood	Yes	His heart was hardened.	The Egyptians worshipped the Nile. Ezek 29:3
Ex 8:1–15	Frogs			
Ex 8:16–19	Gnats			What do the magicians say about God?
Ex 8:20–32	Flies			Israel was not affected.
Ex 9:1–7	Livestock			
Ex 9:8–12	Boils	No		The Lord hardened Pharaoh's heart.
Ex 9:13–35	Hail			Do you believe Pharaoh's response was sincere repentance? (v 27) The land of Goshen was not affected.
Ex 10:1–20	Locusts		Does the Lord accept Pharaoh's compromise?	Servants even told Pharaoh to let the Israelites go.
Ex 10:21–29	Darkness	No		Darkness lasted 3 days, but the people of Israel had light.
Ex 12:1–32	Death of the Firstborn	No		The Israelites were saved if they put the blood of the lamb on the doorpost.

[Author's Note: The Egyptians worshipped many pagan gods. Each of the plagues was a direct attack on the gods of the Egyptians such as Heqet the frog goddess, Uatchit the fly god, etc.]

6. What does Exodus 7:5 indicate was God's intent for the plagues? (For additional insight see 7:17; 9:13, 16, 30; 10:2; 14:4, 18)

7. How does the hardening of Pharaoh's heart have grave consequences for his people?

★ **BONUS Deep Dive:** What pattern do you notice with the hardening of Pharaoh's heart? In each occurrence, who is doing the hardening?

What does it mean that God hardened Pharaoh's heart? See Romans 1:24 for more insight.

8. How was God going to protect the Israelites according to Exodus 12?

Describe the Passover:

How is it significant that God was not going to unilaterally protect each family as he had with the other plagues? How specifically was it determined whether God would protect them?

9. See Exodus 12:40. How was Genesis 15:13-14 fulfilled?

10. How would the celebration of Passover (Exodus 12:43-49) serve as a reminder of their deliverance?

★ **For a Deeper Dive:** How might the Passover and its requirements be a foreshadowing of God's work of redemption in the promised Savior? What do the following verses tell you about the coming Savior? 1 Corinthians 5:7; John 1:29; 1 Peter 1:19; Revelation 5:6; Mark 14:12.

Read: Exodus 13-14 (The parting of the Red Sea)

11. Victory: Describe the Exodus through the Red Sea as recorded in Exodus 14. What was God's battle plan?

12. Describe God's presence with His people? See Exodus 13:21-22.

13. What was the reaction of the Israelites when they witnessed the great power of the Lord?

Read the Song of Moses and Miriam in Exodus 15:1-21. What has God revealed about Himself through the account of the Exodus and these songs?

[Author's Note: Through the deliverance of His people, God keeps all of the promises listed in Exodus 6:1-9. These "I will" statements are also a continuation of the Abrahamic covenant and His promise to bless the nations through a descendant of Abraham.]

SUMMARY WEEK 8

HIStory continues...

Moses confronted the pharaoh: "Let my people go!" But the pharaoh refused. God sent a series of nine plagues on Egypt, each time requesting that the pharaoh let His people go. The nine plagues might seem to the outside eye to be random, but they weren't. Each plague attacked or mocked one of the Egyptian gods. For example, Hapi was a frog goddess of the Egyptians. God sent millions of frogs as one plague. The Egyptian people were helpless to do anything about this plague. They couldn't kill the frogs because they'd be killing their god. The Egyptians depicted both their god Apis and the goddess Hathor as cattle. One plague caused the death of livestock as a judgment against this god and goddess. Through the plagues the God of Israel was shown to be more powerful than any of the many gods of Egypt. They were idols—but He is God. God is still more powerful than any idols of this world.

God sent nine plagues to force the pharaoh's hand, yet God's people remained enslaved. The pharaoh was given many chances to obey God by releasing the Israelites. Each time he refused to obey, his heart hardened, until ultimately, God gave him over to his hardened heart. Then the Lord said to Moses: "Pharaoh's heart is hardened; he refuses to let the people go" (Exodus 7:14). Finally, God said the firstborn sons in all Egypt would die, which would fall on God's people as well. God couldn't let that happen. His people would again need saving.

God showed what it took to be saved from death. He told His people to take a lamb, kill it, and put some of the blood on the top and on both sides of the doorframe to their home. When God saw the blood on a house, He would "pass over" that house, and the firstborn would live. The "blood of the lamb" would be attributed to each person who applied it. Escaping death was not dependent on how good one was. Escaping death was dependent on how faithful one was. Only by accepting God's protection in faith could they be saved.

This was another foreshadowing of the Savior who would come—the Passover Lamb—whose blood would be shed like the ram substituted for Isaac, so that eternal death would be passed over. The people would continue yearly to celebrate the Passover by a sacrifice of an innocent animal. This was in remembrance of God's mercy and grace and what He did for them on that night. He and He alone saved them.

Personal Application

God's purpose in releasing the Israelites was so they could worship him freely. His purpose through the plagues was to remind them who He is. What does this tell you about what God wants from you personally?

The Egyptians served many false gods. While you most likely aren't serving a frog or a river, what false gods are in your own life? In other words, what do you love/adore so much that it turns your affection from God?

How have these false gods proven themselves powerless? How have they left you empty and unfulfilled?

How has God shown Himself more powerful than the false gods in your life?

In order to be saved the Israelites had to apply the blood of the lamb on their doorpost. How does this indicate that faith in God is a personal choice? Have you ever felt like your faith was something you inherited versus something that was your choice? Why or why not?

In Exodus 6:1-8 God explicitly tells the Israelites what He plans to do to deliver them. Clearly we have seen that He is a covenant-keeping God. How does His commitment to His promises encourage you? Which of His promises are you holding to currently?

Additional Notes:

WEEK 9:
The Ten
Commandments

"Moses came and told the people all the words of the Lord and all the rules. And all the people answered with one voice and said, "all the words that the Lord has spoken we will do."

– E X O D U S   2 4 : 3

Scripture: Select passages from Exodus 15:22 through Exodus 20

1. After being freed from bondage, the Israelites found themselves in the desert. It didn't take long before they were grumbling to Moses about their circumstances. What was the choice that God presented to the Israelites? See Exodus 15:25-26.

2. Define grumbling. (Use a dictionary or concordance if needed.)

3. Moses identified their second instance of grumbling for what it was—grumbling against the Lord (Exodus 16:8). What do we learn about complaining from these passages, and how it affects our relationship with God?

4. How did God establish the Sabbath for His people? See Exodus 16:28-30.

5. What does God want them to do with an omer of manna and why? See Exodus 16:31-36.

6. Once again the Israelites complained/grumbled/quarrelled about water (Exodus 17). How did God provide for them?

7. What did God reveal about His character through these chapters? (Particularly as they face seemingly impossible situations.)

8. Read Exodus 19:3-6. Describe the covenant that God made with His people.

9. Fill in the following blanks with words that describe God:

In Egypt, God revealed himself as the _____ of the people. In the desert, God revealed himself as the _____ of the people. In Exodus 20, God presents His people with the 10 commandments or "words" upon which all the laws of Israel would be based. Through these, they will come to know Him as King of the people.

10. Define "commandment."

★ **For a Deeper Dive:** Why did God create the commandments? See Romans 7:7 and Galatians 3:19.

11. What do the first four commandments have in common?

How do the first four commandments set the Israelites apart from other nations?

Commandment 1: How is faithfulness necessary in our relationship with God?

Commandment 2: What does the phrase, "likeness of anything that is in heaven above" (ESV) mean?

Some translations use the term "idol." Define an idol in your own words.

Commandment 3: How do you see this commandment violated today?

Commandment 4: What do you think God's purpose was in establishing the Sabbath? Was it meant to be a burden or a blessing?

12. What do commandments 5 through 10 have in common?

Commandment 5: Define "honor." How does learning to honor our parents help us in our relationship with God? What promise is associated with this command?

Commandments 6-10: Identify each of these commandments:

How does the 10th commandment relate to the others?

How is this sin an affront to God?

13. How are the ten commandments a gift from God? What do they reveal to us about God? What do they reveal to us about ourselves?

SUMMARY WEEK 9

HIStory continues...

God heard the cry of His people and in His grace released them from their bondage. They left Egypt with the Egyptian army pursuing them. When the Israelites came to the Red Sea, with one last miracle, God parted the Red Sea and His people passed through and were rescued. They were then brought to new life on their way to the land that God had promised. Moses met with God on the other side of the Red Sea in Sinai where God established a new order.

God's first covenant, with Adam, had one condition—don't eat the fruit. The Abrahamic Covenant had no conditions and contained God's promises to Abraham—a people, a land, and a mysterious blessing. Now God gave Moses a new covenant that had ten conditions—the Ten Commandments. This covenant was a standard of perfection for God's people and a standard of obedience that God wanted them to meet. The law was to set God's people apart and, through obedience, mark them as His Holy people. It should be remembered that keeping this Mosaic Covenant wouldn't alter the original promise made to Abraham. God would always keep that unconditional promise. The Ten Commandments were part of a conditional covenant. By obeying the laws, God would bless His people, and it would go well for them.

But God knew that His people wouldn't be able to keep the law perfectly. They'd depart from it time and time again. Why then did He give it? In one sense, the law was meant to be a mirror. The people would see in it how far they could depart from the image of God—his blueprint. It was meant to show the Israelites how sinful they were and to reveal the condition of their hearts. But a mirror can only reflect. We don't use mirrors to clean our faces. We need a cleanser for that. God's people, every man and woman, would need a cleanser to rid them of dirt. God revealed in the commandments more of His created intent. The law was meant to show the people how desperately they needed a Savior—a sacrifice—to wash away their sin.

Israel would become God's evidence to the world of His power and His control. If they obeyed, there would be blessings. If they disobeyed, there would be judgment. And it would all happen as God said. It was one thing to establish a plan to redeem; it was another thing for the people to see that they needed the plan at all. God wanted His people to recognize their need for the Savior. Their continual disobedience would accomplish that. If in order to approach God, they needed to obey the law perfectly, then no one—no earthly being—would be able to approach God. The law would demonstrate this, and therefore, God would continually require a blood sacrifice to atone for the people's sins.

The prideful Israelites, however, thought they could do it. They accepted the law rather than cry for mercy. In fact, they responded: "...All that the Lord has spoken we will do." (Exodus 19:8) They believed they could please God on their own, thinking: "I can do this. I can do enough good works. I can be good. I can be perfect." The remainder of the Old Testament illustrates how Israel failed to follow God's perfect law.

Personal Application

Despite God's mighty display of His power in their lives (delivering them from Egypt, parting the Red Sea, etc.), the Israelites still "grumbled" against God and their chosen leaders. They didn't have "remembering hearts." What does this tell you about our own inclination to complain about our circumstances despite God's providence and guidance?

Read Philippians 2:14-16. What light does this verse shed on grumbling or complaining?

What is the opposite of grumbling or complaining? What are some practical ways you can cultivate this habit on a day-to-day basis?

If having eternal life was contingent on being able to keep all the commandments, would you be able to keep them? Why or why not?

Are there any commandments that you struggle obeying? Why or why not?

As we continue with HIStory, we will learn that due to the sacrifice of the promised Savior Christ, we are no longer declared righteous by observing the Law (Romans 3:20; Galatians 2:16; Ephesians 2:8-9), and yet we are called to obey its requirements (Matthew 22:37-40). What benefit is there for us to follow the Law? Consider Psalms 119:113-120, 151-152, 160.

★ **For a Deeper Dive:** Read Matthew 22:36–40. How does this verse show that the Promised Savior will affirm the heart of the law? (For additional insight see Matt 5:17)

Additional Notes:

WEEK 10:
Call to Worship

"Then all the congregation raised a loud cry, and the people wept that night. And all the people of Israel grumbled against Moses and Aaron. The whole congregation said to them, "Would that we had died in the land of Egypt! Or would that we had died in this wilderness! Why is the Lord bringing us into this land, to fall by the sword? Our wives and our little ones will become a prey. Would it not be better for us to go back to Egypt?"

- N U M B E R S   1 4 : 1 - 3

Scripture: Selected passages from Exodus 25–40, Leviticus & Numbers

Read Exodus 25: 1-9

1. As discussed in last week's lesson, grumbling is an affront to God. God wanted His people to come into His presence and worship Him with a grateful heart. What do you learn about giving to the Lord from Exodus 25:1-7? How is giving a part of worship to the Lord?

2. What was the purpose of the sanctuary that the Israelites were to make? (See Exodus 25:8)

3. How is it significant to you that God wants a place to dwell with His people?

4. What are the benefits of being in the presence of God? See Psalm 16:11.

Read Exodus 26–30

The Tabernacle

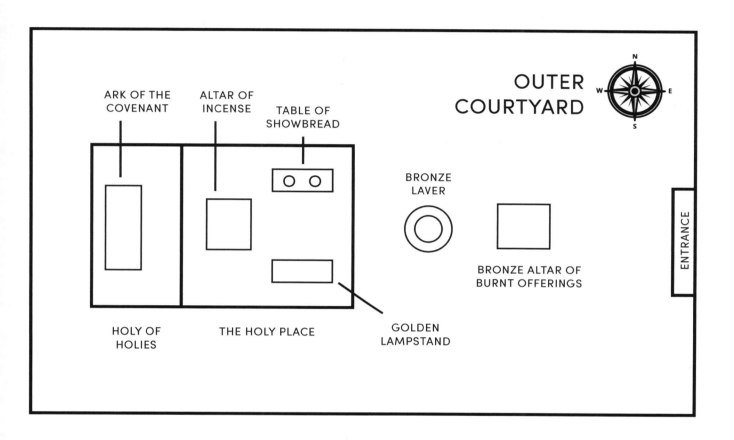

5. Look at the layout of the tabernacle. How many entrances were there?

What does the number of entrances imply about entering into the presence of God?

⭐ **For a Deeper Dive:** Read & consider John 10:9.

6. Read Exodus 29:35-37. How would the shedding of blood remind the Israelites of the severity of their sin? (For additional insight see Leviticus 22:17-31).

Define atonement. Use a bible dictionary or concordance if necessary.

What do you learn about the relationship between atonement and coming into God's presence from these verses?

7. Leviticus 16 describes the Day of Atonement. What do verses 29-34 say is the purpose of this holy day?

8. Read Exodus 32:1-6. What commandments were broken by the Israelites when they built the golden calf? How did Moses intercede for the people? See Exodus 32:11-16.

9. In Exodus 33:18-23, Moses asked God, "Please show me your glory." What was God's response to the request of Moses?

10. What did God proclaim about His name as He passed by Moses? See Exodus 34:6-7. What did Moses request of God in verse 9?

11. God renewed His covenant with His people and gave them positive instructions to help them walk in obedience (Exodus 34:10-27). He also promised them that His Presence would go with them as they continued their journey to the Promised Land. How did this demonstrate His grace and love for His people?

[Author's note: The tabernacle was built by the people "as the Lord had commanded Moses." Exodus and Leviticus established the laws of obedience, as well as the roles of the Priests who would intercede for them. God wanted His people to serve and worship Him alone. If obedient, His presence would be with them. Blood sacrifices would be necessary to atone for their sins and God's presence would be restored. They were a freed people, but they still had to travel to the Promised Land. For a look ahead into HIStory, see Hebrews 9.]

How would the people know of God's presence as they journeyed to the Promised Land? See Exodus 40:34-38.

12. Despite God's promises of blessings, the people continued to sin and grumble. Numbers 13-14 describes events that took place when they reached the brink of entering the Promised Land. What was God's judgment? See Numbers 14:26-38.

Who from the original generation entered the Promised Land?

Do you think God's judgment was harsh? Why or why not?

13. Write down all the miracles the Israelites have experienced thus far. How do these events demonstrate His care and provision for His people, despite His judgement?

SUMMARY WEEK 10

HIStory continues...

God gave the law—the Ten Commandments—and Exodus records that He also provided a place His people could meet with Him. It was to be the tabernacle, a tent that would move with the people as they traveled to the Promised Land. It was to be constructed exactly as God prescribed.

Later, a structure, the Temple, would be built in Jerusalem with the same physical components as the tabernacle. Both the tabernacle and the Temple symbolized God's presence and would be temporary provisions for God's people. They were a foreshadowing of a permanent dwelling place for God. Someday, God would dwell in the hearts of man and woman.God is holy and His presence requires the cleansing of sin. God gave man and woman this opportunity. Within the tabernacle, and later the Temple, the high priest made a sacrifice by substituting the life of an innocent unblemished animal in exchange for the sin of man and woman. As the people would continue to sin, the blood of the innocents would be shed over and over again. God wanted them to see that their sin had grave consequences—it separated them from Him. While this was God's temporary plan and provision for reconciliation, it foreshadowed the hope of a permanent atonement. One day, Satan would receive the fatal bruise to his head through the sacrifice and suffering of Eve's offspring, a Savior, who would come through the line of Abraham. Evil would be banished, as God had intended.

It was in LEVITICUS where God established that the people would need an intercessor, or high priest, to approach God on their behalf and to make their sacrifices. The priest would come from the tribe of Levi. Of course, there was a problem. The priests themselves were not without sin and would first have to make atonement for their own sins. An imperfect priest was a temporary provision that pointed to the promise of a perfect high priest to come—one without sin. God reminded His people they were to worship Him. Those redeemed, those who atoned through the system of sacrifice, could come into His Holy presence.The promises of God had to be fulfilled. After all, God promised.

So where are we in God's plan? The people had escaped Egypt, they were numerous, but they didn't yet possess the land that God had promised. The Land of Canaan was in the possession of pagan nations. The Israelites needed to travel from Sinai to Canaan. During this time, the people demonstrated that they still couldn't keep the law, they were complainers, they were rebellious, and they didn't respond to God's grace with gratitude. On their own, they couldn't approach God. But God faithfully led them as they continued on their journey to the Promised Land.

In the book of NUMBERS, we read that when they were on the brink of the land God had promised to Abraham, they sent out spies to look over the land they would possess. Two spies, Joshua and Caleb, claimed the land to be ready for God to take. But ten of the spies reported giants in the land. The people were overwhelmed and afraid, agreeing with the majority that it was too dangerous to enter. Because of their unfaithfulness, God ordained forty years of additional wilderness wanderings for His people. Only the two obedient men—Joshua and Caleb—would be allowed to enter the Promised Land with the next generation.

Personal Application

This portion of HIStory describes the importance of obedience & worshiping God. Define worship. Use a dictionary or concordance if needed.

Read Psalm 95.

Based on where we are in HIStory, and from this psalm, what do you learn about worship? Where and how can you worship God?

1 Samuel 12:24 says, "Only fear the Lord and serve him faithfully with all your heart. For consider what great things he has done for you." What great things has God done for you? Why is it important to have a heart that remembers what He has done?

To worship the Lord, what posture should our hearts have before Him? (Reread Psalm 95 for insight.)

Describe how you worship God.

God gave the Israelites very clear instructions on building the tabernacle so that He could dwell with them and provide them a place of worship. What does it mean to you to be in God's presence? Where do you experience His presence?

What distractions or sins in our lives can prevent you from worshipping God wholeheartedly? List some of them below.

Additional Notes:

WEEK 11:
Joshua Now Leads

"...But as for me and my house, we will serve the Lord."

- J O S H U A   2 4 : 1 5

Scripture: Select passages from Numbers, Deuteronomy & Joshua

1. Read Numbers 20:7-12. Why did God forbid Moses from leading the people into the Promised Land?

[Author's Note: The word "Deuteronomy" comes from the Greek word for "the second law" or "the law copied or repeated." In the book of Deuteronomy Moses wrote a series of three speeches to the people of Israel before they were to enter the land of Canaan, the Promised Land. While Moses would not lead them into the Land, he wanted to remind them of God's law, and everything that God did for them. He wanted them to remember every promise God made to them. Moses explained to them that their new life in the land of Canaan would be blessed or cursed depending on their ability to walk after God and keep His law. His words were spoken in the final year of wanderings in the wilderness.]

2. Read the following passages. Sum up Moses' reminders to the Israelites.

SCRIPTURE	REMINDER
Deuteronomy 4:1-8	
Deuteronomy 4:15-19	
Deuteronomy 5:6-21	
Deuteronomy 7:6-11	
Deuteronomy 7:17-19	
Deuteronomy 8:1-2, 19-20	
Deuteronomy 11:1-7, 26-28	
Deuteronomy 30:15-16	

3. The death of Moses is recorded in Deuteronomy 34. What do you learn about Moses from verses 9-12?

How is this description of Moses ironic considering what he struggled with in Week 7?

Read Joshua 1–4

4. What were the Lord's commands to Joshua as recorded in Joshua 1:1-9?

What was the Lord's promise to Joshua?

5. ★ **For a Deeper Dive:** Read the story of Rahab in Joshua 2. What is significant about her? See Matthew 1:5 for additional insight.

6. Consider that it was over forty years since the Israelites were freed from bondage to the Egyptians. They were finally about to enter the Promised Land by crossing the Jordan River. Describe what they may have been feeling.

How did God assure them of HIs presence? See Joshua 3:1-6.

7. What was the first thing that the Israelites did after crossing the Jordan? See Joshua 4:1-10. What was the significance of their act?

8. Joshua 6 begins the account of the military campaigns to gain the Promised Land from the pagan nations. Read the account of Jericho in Joshua 6. What role did the Ark of the Covenant play?

[Author's Note: The Lord ordered the total destruction of the city and all that was in it. Several things should be noted to help us understand this command. First, God's command for total destruction only applied to land within the Promised Land (Deuteronomy 20:16-18). Second, God was establishing a theocracy for His people and He wanted the people to remain pure and free from foreign idols and pagan worship (Deuteronomy 7:1-6). Third, the Bible and historical records document that the Canaanites were a debase and evil culture. Finally, consider that God waited 400 years to bring judgment upon the Canaanites. At any time they could have turned from their evil practices.]

9. What do you learn about the Canaanites and their behaviors from Deut 12:30-31? (For additional insight see Leviticus 18:24-26; Leviticus 18:30; Deuteronomy 18:9-11.)

10. What do you learn about God from the following verses:

    a. Psalm 145:8

    b. 2 Peter 3:9

11. What do you learn about God's provisions from Joshua 6:27?

Where else have you seen this promise in HIStory so far?

12. What does Joshua 11:23 indicate is given to the Israelites as an inheritance?

How does this inheritance affirm God's promise to Abraham and his descendants?

13. ★ **For a Deeper Dive:** The tribes were commanded to go in and possess their allotted land. Their inheritance was contingent on their obedience and faith that God would equip them for the task. The inheritance of land was meant to be a foreshadowing of the eternal inheritance that we are promised. (Keep this in mind as HIStory unfolds.) Given the idea of an inheritance, consider Ephesians 1:11-14; Ephesians 3:6; 1 Peter 1:3-4. What do these verses tell you about the promise of a future inheritance?

14. Summarize Joshua's closing remarks in Joshua 24:14-28. Considering all that the Lord had done for them, do you believe these commands were just and fair?

15. Read Joshua 24:1-13. Count how many times "I" is used by the Lord. What was God reminding the Israelites as they appropriated the Promised Land?

SUMMARY WEEK 11

HIStory continues...

In the book of Numbers, God recounts the wanderings of His people. The people continued grumbling about their circumstances. Moses became angry with them, but rather than trusting God to deal with His people, he sinned and disobeyed God. Therefore, God determined that Moses would not lead the people into the Promised Land.

As righteous as Moses was—he was, after all, a deliverer of his people—he wasn't the one promised. What better way to demonstrate that he wasn't the promised Savior than to forbid Moses from entering the Promised Land? God chose Joshua, instead, to lead the people. Moses gave a wonderful encouraging speech to the people to again remind them of God's promise of future blessings. It's recorded in DEUTERONOMY.

God's promises were still preserved. A descendant of Abraham would one day bless the nations of the world. In order to recognize Him and in order to prove that He was the promised Savior, the genealogical record of Abraham's family would have to be kept. It was.

The history of God's chosen people continues with Joshua leading the people into the land, so the second of God's promises to Abraham would be kept. God vowed that He would be with Joshua on this journey: "Have I not commanded you? Be strong and courageous. Do not be frightened, and do not be dismayed, for the Lord your God is with you wherever you go" (Joshua 1:9). God would always be with His people.

God led the people across the Jordan River and into the Promised Land. Because the land was occupied by pagan nations, the Lord directed Joshua in several military campaigns to take over the land. His protection was obvious. One of the most well-known instances called for Joshua to lead a march with trumpets around the city of Jericho for six days. On the seventh day, the walls of the city came down and God's people were able to capture the city. God's direction and Joshua's obedience are recorded in the book called JOSHUA.

The land was not yet fully conquered near the end of Joshua's life. In faith, however, Joshua divided the land between the tribes of Israel, with the exception of the priestly tribe of Levi. The designation was the recognition of their inheritance and God's promise of land. The descendants of Joseph, the favored son who rescued the people many years earlier, were given two shares of land represented by his two sons. The tribes were commanded to conquer the pagan people occupying the land. God would give them victory if they obeyed Him. As God's people entered and overtook the various nations, He wanted them to rid the land of the pagan and evil practices. He wanted them to worship Him alone. Life in this land wouldn't be easy for God's people, but God again promised blessings for obedience and consequences for disobedience.

SUMMARY

Under the leadership of Joshua, the people of Israel served the Lord and not idols. And just like Joseph, the bones of Joshua were buried in the Promised Land. Joshua was the model of a faithful servant of God. Before he died, Joshua reminded the people of God's Mosaic covenant and the personal choice each could make. God made it clear, as He did in the Garden, that man and woman had free choice, and the freedom to choose the consequences of serving self rather than God.

Personal Application

Both Moses and Joshua reminded the Israelites to not stray from the Lord and His commandments. Considering their instruction, what are practical ways that you can cultivate obedience to the Lord's commandments?

Joshua 1:9b says, "the Lord your God is with you wherever you go." Later we see the Ark of the Covenant literally guiding the way into the Promised Land. How is God's promise of guidance comforting to you?

How has God guided you?

When approaching the Jordan, the Israelites had to step into the rushing water before it parted. Where might God be calling you to step out in faith?

The Israelites faced three obstacles initially to entering the Promised Land (spying out Jericho, crossing the Jordan, defeating Jericho). What obstacles do you face in claiming God's promises?

Additional Notes:

WEEK 12:
Ruth Chooses God

"...Your people shall be my people, and your God my God. Where you die I will die, and there will I be buried. May the Lord do so to me and more also if anything but death parts me from you."

– RUTH 1:16-17

Scripture: Select passages from Joshua, Judges and Ruth

1. Read Joshua's previous charge to the leaders of Israel in Joshua 23:4-13. Now read Judges 1:27-2:15. How were the tribes of Israel disobedient after the death of Joshua?

2. What was the consequence for their disobedience?

3. Read Judges 2:16-23. What do you learn about the Judges the Lord raised up?

4. A cycle of events is repeated over and over in this portion of HIStory. Identify the cycle events:

    a. From Judges 2:11; 3:7, 12; 4:1; 6:1; 10:6; 13:1

        The people of Israel did _____

    b. From Judges 2:14; 3:8; 4:2; 6:1b; 10:7; 13:1b

        So the Lord _____

    c. From Judges 3:9a, 15; 4:3; 6:7; 10:10

        Then the people _____

    d. From Judges 3:9b, 15; 4:4

        The Lord raised raised up for them a _____

    [Author's note: The oppression caused by the enemies occupying the land was allowed by God due to the disobedience of God's people. The Judges were not necessarily actual judges as we understand the word. They were deliverers who were raised up by God to bring relief to the oppression.]

5. The cycle noted above occurs thirteen times in the book of Judges. What does the cyclical nature of sin reveal about the people of Israel?

What does it reveal about the condition of the heart of man?

What does it reveal about God?

Scripture: Ruth

(The narrative of Ruth takes place during the period of the Judges.)

Read Ruth 1

6. From Ruth 1:1-5, what do you learn about Ruth, Orpah and Naomi? What were their respective nationalities? Why was Naomi in Moab?

7. Why did Naomi decide to leave Moab, and where did she determine to go?

8. Naomi encouraged her daughters-in-law to go back to their families and remain in Moab. What were their decisions?

What was the reason that Ruth gave as why she would go with Naomi?

9. What did Ruth relinquish when she decided to go with Naomi? What do you think she gained by her decision?

⭐ **For a Deeper Dive:** Ruth says, "your God will be my God" indicating that she is choosing Yahweh over her own pagan god(s). What does Acts 11:18 tell you about adoption into God's family?

10. Read Ruth 2–4. In your own words describe the relationship between Naomi and her daughter-in-law, Ruth?

What do you learn about Ruth's character?

[Author's Note: According to the law given to Moses, if a poor man was forced to sell his property, his relative could buy back the property by paying the ransom. He was considered a "kinsman redeemer." Additionally, if a man died without an heir, a kinsman could marry the widow and raise a son to hand down his name (Deuteronomy 25:5; Leviticus 25). This was a provision in the law which provided for the widow, and this is what Naomi referenced in Ruth 2:20. The book of Ruth provides a narrative regarding the application of this law—Naomi instructed Ruth as to how she could procure Boaz, a wealthy relative, to be Ruth's kinsman redeemer. As HIStory unfolds you will see how the promised Savior would fill the role of our Redeemer!]

11. Despite that there was a closer heir (Ruth 3:12), how did Boaz procure Ruth to be his wife as recorded in Chapter 4?

12. Considering Ruth's declaration in Ruth 1:16-17, how did God bless her dedication and faithfulness?

13. List the heirs of Boaz. Keep his lineage in mind as HIStory unfolds.

SUMMARY WEEK 12

HIStory Continues...

The government in the new land was a theocracy. God was their ruler, guide, and king. God gave the people judges, righteous men who would lead as the people began to occupy the Promised Land. Life under the judges is recorded in the book named JUDGES.

The events of Judges demonstrated the cycle of sin. As soon as a judge died, the people would again disobey. God would then punish the Israelites by delivering them into the hands of a different nation. That would lead to repentance, and God would ordain a new judge. There were thirteen cycles of this and a total of fourteen judges. It's quite tiresome reading this account of the people. Why couldn't the Israelites learn from their past sins?

God was showing them that they couldn't approach Him on their own. God wanted His people to realize they were to be a people set apart—holy—and separate from the pagan practices of the world. He would always have this same desire for His creation. Yet again and again, they were disobedient. They always needed rescuing.

The story of RUTH is the story of one life under the rule of the judges and another story of redemption. Ruth was from one of the pagan nations, Moab. The Moabites worshiped the pagan god, Chemosh. Historical records indicate that this god required such practices as human sacrifice. His very name means "destroyer." During a famine in Israel, a man and his wife, Naomi, along with two sons went to live in Moab. After the man died, his sons married Moabite women, Ruth and Orpah. After about ten years, the sons also died. Without a husband or sons, Naomi chose to return to her people when she'd heard there was no longer a famine. Ruth chose to accompany her mother-in-law back to the land of God's people. Ruth pledged to worship the God of Israel and her faithful service was blessed. She married Boaz, a wealthy Israelite, who is part of the line of Abraham. Ruth would become the great-grandmother of King David. It would be from the line of David that God would further identify the one promised long ago. And the Savior would come from the offspring of Ruth.

Personal Application

In this period of HIStory, we see the Israelites continually choose sin over God. It's easy to see their behavior and think how did they not get it? Yet when we look at our own heart we may see the same likelihood to get stuck in the cycle of sin. Consider the words of the ancient hymn, Come Thou Fount:

"Oh to grace how great a debtor
Daily I'm constrained to be!
Let Thy goodness, like a fetter
Bind my wandering heart to Thee.
Prone to wander, Lord, I feel it,
Prone to leave the God I love;
Here's my heart, O take and seal it,
Seal it for Thy courts above."

— ROBERT ROBINSON, 1757

When are you most tempted (or most likely) to wander from the Lord? What can you do to "return to the Lord" or "bind [your] wandering heart" to Him?

Despite their sin, God sent deliverers to rescue the Israelites. What does this reality tell you about God's commitment to save (or redeem) His people?

Both the Israelites and Ruth had to "choose on this day whom you will serve" (Joshua 24:15). When in your life have you been at a crossroads to either choose God or an alternative? How did you respond?

Ruth's decision to follow the God of Israel was influenced by her relationship with her mother-in-law, Naomi. Has there been a person in your life who has taught you about God, either in words or actions? How has he/she influenced your life?

Is there someone in your sphere of influence who God may be calling you to share about God? Is there someone that you can be a Naomi to?

Imagine going from an outcast to a redeemed participant in society. Write a short prayer of thanksgiving representing how you might feel towards the one who saved you.

Additional Notes:

WEEK 13:
Saul is King

"...But there shall be a king over us, that we also may be like all the nations, and that our king may judge us and go out before us and fight our battles."

-1 SAMUEL 8:19-20

Scripture: Select passages from 1 Samuel.

[Author's Note: During this time in HIStory there were enemies around Israel who threatened the people and their land. God had established a Theocracy where He would be their King and there would be blessings and fruitfulness if they obeyed. He would protect them if they chose to worship Him and submit to His perfect and loving Kingship. Choosing disobedience, however, would have consequences—God would withdraw His protection. It was always their choice.]

1. Read the account of Samuel's birth in 1 Samuel 1–2:11. What do you learn about Hannah from these passages? How is Hannah an example to follow?

2. What do you learn about prayer from Hannah?

3. What did Hannah do in 1 Samuel 1:21-27? (See Numbers 6 and Leviticus 27:1-8 for additional insight.) What more do you learn about Hannah?

4. For what positions did the Lord call Samuel? See 1 Samuel 3:20 and 7:15.

5. All prophets in the Old Testament shared certain characteristics. Consider the following:

    a. A prophet had to be _____ by the Lord. (1 Samuel 3:4)

    b. The Lord revealed Himself to the prophet by _____ (1 Samuel 3:21)

    c. The prophet told _____ to the people. (1 Samuel 8:10)

    d. All that the prophet says _____ (1 Samuel 9:6)

[Author's Note: We will see other prophets throughout HIStory. They were chosen by God to communicate His message to the people. While they came from different backgrounds, they were all called to deliver God's message accurately. Some prophets told the people of future events that would take place in the near or distant future.]

6. Read 1 Samuel 8:5, 19–20. What did the Israelites ask of Samuel? What was their stated reason?

7. Samuel prayed to the Lord, and the Lord responded. What was the Lord's reply?

8. Summarize the warning that Samuel gave to the people in 1 Samuel 8:10–18.

★ **For a Deeper Dive:** Consider all the things that you have learned about God thus far. How does God as King differ from the king of the world as described by Samuel?

9. God granted the people's request for a king, although He wanted to be their King. What does God's response teach you about God?

10. What do you learn about Saul from 1 Samuel 9:1–2?

11. The Lord anointed Saul to be king. Samuel gave a final charge to the people of Israel in 1 Samuel 12. What did Samuel remind them to do in verses 14-16?

12. Examine the following events of Saul's kingship to determine how well he followed the commands of the Lord.

SCRIPTURE	THE LORD'S COMMAND	SAUL'S DISOBEDIENCE
1 Samuel 10:8; 13:8-15		

1 Samuel 15:1-21
(See Exodus 17:8-16 for an
understanding of God's command.)

13. The Lord had anointed Saul king because the people wanted a king. Saul had all the worldly attributes that the people wanted. Why then did the Lord discontinue the kingdom of Saul? See 1 Samuel 13:13-14 and 15:10-11.

14. Read 1 Samuel 15:22-23. Why is obedience to the Lord better than sacrifice?

SUMMARY WEEK 13

HIStory Continues...

The last judge was Samuel. There are two books of this history named for him—I and II SAMUEL. Samuel was not only a judge but also a prophet of God.

The Israelites became dissatisfied with the theocracy God had established. Essentially, they declared—We want to be like everyone else. The rest of the nations had kings. The Israelites wanted to unite all the tribes as one nation under the rule of a king. God's desire was that they be distinguished from the other nations. It wasn't that God objected to a new system of government for the people—He would soon select a human king of His choosing for them—but He wanted them to wait on His timing. God's desire for them would be that they worship Him and seek guidance from Him alone. And He wanted their human king to submit to His authority. God would be King of kings. Unfortunately, the Israelite's demand for a king demonstrated that they didn't want God to rule over them at all.

Though God warned them, through Samuel, that a king wasn't a good idea, in His permissive will He honored their request. God had one provision—worship Me and Me alone. All would still be well in the land if the people and their king worshiped Him. If they didn't, there would be judgment and consequences for turning away. (Again, nothing would affect the unconditional promise to Abraham of a people, a land, and a blessing.)

Saul, the first king of the Israelites, was strong, handsome, and from a good family. He wasn't "humanly" inferior, quite the opposite. God gave the people what they wanted—a king like the world's kings. But Saul didn't seek God's direction and purpose. From the beginning of his monarchy, he and the people didn't honor God. Samuel tried to warn Saul, but his warnings were ignored and the Israelites suffered due to Saul's sinfulness. God was demonstrating that His blessings would only come from obedience.

Personal Application

Consider how Hannah took the longings of her heart before God. Is there anything that you are longing for?

Psalm 107:9 says "For he satisfies the longing soul, and the hungry soul he fills with good things." How can you practically look to God to fulfill the longings of your soul like Hannah did?

Reread this week's key verse. By whose moral authority do you find it is easier to live by—God's or the world's? Why?

Can you think of activities that are okay with our world's system of morality or righteousness, but are against God's Word? Have you ever struggled with a decision to be "like the nations" rather than to submit to God as King? Explain.

Additional Notes:

WEEK 14:
David is Anointed

"The Lord is my shepherd; I shall not want. He makes me lie down in green pastures. He leads me beside still waters. He restores my soul. He leads me in paths of righteousness for His name's sake. Even though I walk through the valley of the shadow of death, I will fear no evil, for you are with me; your rod and your staff, they comfort me. You prepare a table before me in the presence of my enemies; you anoint my head with oil; my cup overflows. Surely goodness and mercy shall follow me all the days of my life, and I shall dwell in the house of the lord forever."

– PSALM 23

Scripture: Select passages from 1st and 2nd Samuel

[Author's Note: This week's study will focus on the key events of the life of David. David was the king of God's choosing, who was anointed to rule Israel and fight its enemies. Through David, God revealed more of how the promise he made to David would be fulfilled. David is also credited with writing many of the Psalms. Through the Psalms we learn about the heart of the man that God chose and the heart that God desires for us all.]

David as a shepherd:

1. Read 1 Samuel 16:1-13. What do you learn about David?

What do you learn from this passage as to why God selected him to be the next king?

2. When David is brought in before Samuel, what does God tell the Prophet to do to David?

[Author's Note: The Hebrew for the word anoint (mashach) means to smear or rub with oil, which was symbolic for God's blessing or call upon a person's life. In the case with David, he was consecrated, or set apart for a special purpose in God's plan. Later in HIStory we'll see that the Promised Savior was also anointed and set apart for a special purpose.]

3. List the things that a shepherd must do. How may David's life as a shepherd have prepared him to be king? See Psalm 23 for additional insight.

4. Read 1 Samuel 16:14-23. What do you learn about David?

5. Why was Saul looking for a musician? Why did he select David, and what was their initial relationship like?

Read 1 Samuel 17, the story of David and Goliath. What do you learn about David's character from this account?

What was his motivation to fight Goliath?

What does he say when Goliath taunts him?

How may his experience with Goliath prepared the young David to be king?

6. Read 1 Samuel 18:6-30. What happened to the relationship between Saul and David? Why?

David as a Fugitive

7. Saul's initial attempt to kill David is recorded in 1 Samuel 19-20. During this time, David wrote Psalm 59. Read through the Psalm. List all of the things that David knew (and recited) about God.

8. What do you learn about David's heart from Psalm 59?

9. Read 1 Samuel 24. What do you learn about David's character?

   Do you think Saul was repentant? See 1 Samuel 26:1-5 for insight.

10. Consider all that David endured before becoming king—he became an enemy of King Saul; he was pursued to be killed; he was exiled from his homeland; he took refuge in enemy territory; his wives were captured, and finally his own people spoke of stoning him. How did David endure all of his suffering? See 1 Samuel 30:6.

11. How did Saul die? See 1 Samuel 31:1-7.

   [Author's Note: In 2 Samuel 1, an Amalekite takes responsibility for the death of Saul. This would seem like a contradiction with the account in 1 Samuel 31. Most scholars believe, however, that the Amalekite man lied in order to receive a benefit or reward for causing Saul's death. Also it is the narrator (the inspired recorder of Scripture) in 1 Samuel who gave the account of Saul's death. In the second account nowhere does it state that the Amalekite did kill Saul—only that the Amalekite said he did.]

12. David laments over the death of Saul, and his son (David's loyal friend), Jonathan. What does his grief tell you about the heart of David?

David as King

13. How did David become king over the tribe of Judah? See 2 Samuel 2:1-4.

    How did he become king over all the tribes of Israel? See 2 Samuel 5:1-5.

14. As king, David returned the ark of the covenant to Jerusalem. As a refresher, what was the ark of the covenant, and what did it represent? See Exodus 25:10-22.

15. What observation did David make to Nathan the prophet in 2 Samuel 7:1-2? (This is also recorded in 1 Chronicles 17:1.)

16. ★ **For a Deeper Dive:** Read God's response in 2 Samuel 7:8-17. When David told God that he wanted to build God a house, he was talking about a temple to house the ark where the priests would offer sacrifices and mediate between God and His people. What kind of house was God talking about?

    How does God's response further expand the promise given to Abraham?

What do we learn from this prophecy about the lineage of the coming Savior? [Keep this prophecy of the Savior's lineage in mind as HIStory unfolds: the promised One will come from the tribe of Judah!]

[Author's Note: To understand all that God promised here to David, we have to understand that this prophecy did what a lot of prophetic messages in the Old Testament did. They spoke of events that would be fulfilled in Israel's near future, as well as in the distant future. They took an extended series of events and collapsed them so that the near and distant events could appear to be only one event. In next week's lesson we will see that the near future fulfillment of the building of the physical Temple occurred under the reign of Solomon, David's son.]

17. David was a successful king. He won battles and "administered justice and equity to all his people" (2 Samuel 8:15). He was not without sin, however. David's well-known transgressions are recorded in 2 Samuel 11–12, where we learn that he committed adultery with another man's wife, and then plotted to have the husband killed!

    Read Psalm 51. What do you learn about repentance from this psalm David wrote?

18. What reasons are given in Scripture as to why David would not be the one to build the Temple, but rather the commission would be given to his son, Solomon? See 1 Chronicles 22:8 and 28:3-8. What does this insight reveal about God?

SUMMARY WEEK 14

HIStory Continues...

The second king was David, chosen by God's prophet Samuel. David was the eighth and youngest son of Jesse from the tribe of Judah. By the world's standards, the fact that David was the youngest son and was also a shepherd would have seemed to make him a surprising choice.

Although chosen by God's servant, the path to kingship wasn't easy for David. For more than fifteen years God trained David through many trials and tribulations. King Saul wasn't going to give up the throne without a fight, and David became a fugitive, fleeing in order to escape Saul's wrath. David had the opportunity to kill Saul, but waited for God's timing to become king.

After the death of King Saul, David was anointed. He first ruled over just the house of his own tribe and later over all Israel. During the period of King David's reign, the nation flourished and conquered its enemies. Israel became the envy of the nations surrounding it.

David was the primary author of the PSALMS. Throughout his songs, he expressed his honest fears of danger during his trials, but he boldly declared that his only hope was in God. David was far from a perfect man. He committed adultery with Bathsheba and then murdered her husband. He always repented and grieved over his sins. He expressed his desire that God search his heart: "Search me, O God, and know my heart! Try me and know my thoughts! And see if there be any grievous way in me, and lead me in the way everlasting!" (Psalm 139:23–24). So God, who looks on the heart of man, referred to David as "a man after God's own heart."

From David's lineage, God would further narrow the promise made hundreds of years earlier to Abraham. Through the prophet Nathan, God promised David: "When your days are fulfilled and you lie down with your fathers, I will raise up your offspring after you, who shall come from your body, and I will establish his kingdom. He shall build a house for my name, and I will establish the throne of his kingdom forever" (2 Samuel 7:12–13). David was a foreshadowing of the Savior to come. God had promised that the Savior would come from the offspring of David, from the line of Judah, and one day, He would reign forever.

Personal Application

What do you think it means that "David strengthened himself in the Lord his God"? How can you strengthen yourself in the Lord?

Consider the following reference to David in the New Testament: "...I have found in David the son of Jesse a man after my heart, who will do all my will. Of this man's offspring God has brought to Israel a Savior, Jesus, as he promised" (Acts 13:22-23). Why did God refer to David as "a man after my heart"?

List some practical ways that we can we cultivate a heart that seeks after God's heart? From your list, circle one thing you can implement this week.

Carefully consider Psalm 23, our passage for the week. How have you experienced the Lord as your shepherd?

What attributes of God, listed in the Psalm, are particularly meaningful to you?

How can Psalm 23 encourage you in times of trouble?

Additional Notes:

WEEK 15:
Solomon Now Reigns

"...Have you considered my servant Job, that there is none like him on the earth, a blameless and upright man, who fears God and turns away from evil."

- J O B   2 : 3 A

Scripture: Select passages from 1st & 2nd Kings, 1st & 2nd Chronicles, Ecclesiastes, Proverbs, the Song of Solomon, and Job

1. What do you learn about the third and final king of the united kingdom of Israel from the following verses?

    a. 1 Kings 1:28-31

    b. 1 Kings 2:1-4, 10-12

    c. 1 Kings 3:1-15

2. Define wisdom in your own words.

    What is the difference between knowledge and wisdom?

3. ★ **For a Deeper Dive:** Solomon has been accredited with writing the books of Proverbs, and Song of Solomon. What do you learn about wisdom from the following passages?

   a. Proverbs 1:5

   b. Proverbs 1:7

   c. Proverbs 3:7-8

   d. Proverbs 4:4

   e. Proverbs 8:13-14

   f. Song of Solomon 2:7; 6:3

[Author's Note: There are various interpretations of the Song of Solomon in Scripture. It presents events and feelings in the days leading up to and during marriage. It provides encouragement toward the goal of lasting love, purity and holiness within the marriage. It expresses the warning that women should wait for love (2:7; 3:5; 8:4) and declares the beauty of sexual union within a marriage.]

4. How do we see God answer Solomon's request for wisdom in the following verses:

    a. 1 Kings 3:16-28

    b. 1 Kings 4:20-25, 29-34

    c. 1 Kings 10:1-13

    d. 1 Kings 10:23-25

5. Solomon was given the task of building the Temple. What was the Lord's command regarding the Temple? See 1 Kings 6:11-13.

6. While the Temple was the designated place for the people to meet God and atone for their sins, Solomon recognized that God could not be contained in one place. What do you learn about God from Solomon's prayer in 1 Kings 8:27-30?

7. Summarize the Lord's warning to Solomon in 1 Kings 9:1-9.

8. How did Solomon turn from the Lord? See 1 Kings 11:1-8.

★ For a Deeper Dive: How is it possible that Solomon had more wisdom than anyone, but could still turn from the Lord?

9. What was the consequence for his disobedience? See 1 Kings 11:9-13.

Solomon most likely wrote Ecclesiastes during the end of his life. Compare Ecclesiastes 2:11 with 12:13-14. What does Solomon conclude at the end of his life?

Scripture: Job

[Author's Note: The author of the book of Job is not given in Scripture. Some scholars have theorized that it was written by Moses, others by Solomon, and some by Job himself. Historically, the story of Job most likely took place much earlier (perhaps during the period of Genesis). However, since the book is considered a "wisdom" book it is included in this week's lesson.]

10. What do you learn about Job's character in verse 1:1? What do each of these descriptors mean?

11. Read Job 1:6-12. What is the challenge that God gave to Satan?

What limit does God put on Satan?

What does this tell you about God?

12. Read through Job 1:13-2:10. What did Satan do to Job?

What was Job's response?

13. What is the reason his friends gave for his suffering? See Job 22:5-10. Were they correct?

14. After some time, Job began to question why God would allow suffering on his life. What is God's response to Job's doubt? See Job 38:1-4.

Does God give a reason for Job's suffering? What does God's response tell us about God? Suffering?

Read Job 42:1-6. What was Job's final response to the Lord?

★ **For a Deeper Dive:** Job poses several prophetic questions whose answers will be revealed by the coming of the promised Savior. Record these questions below. What might they tell us about the Savior and what He will accomplish?

Job 14:4 (For additional insight see Hebrews 10:14; Colossians 1:21-23; 2 Corinthians 5:17)

Job 14:10

Job 14:14 (For additional insight see 1 Corinthians 15:54-55)

SUMMARY WEEK 15

HIStory continues...

There was one last king of the united kingdom of Israel. He was David's son, Solomon. God had given Solomon great wisdom. While it's uncertain whether he wrote or merely collected the writings in PROVERBS, ECCLESIASTES, and THE SONG OF SOLOMON, the timeless wisdom recorded in these books of literature speaks of the benefit and blessings of relying solely on God for direction and instruction. "Trust in the Lord with all your heart, and do not lean on your own understanding" (Proverbs 3:5).

During Solomon's reign, the nation grew in wealth, and among other nations, it grew in stature. God ordained Solomon to build His Temple. It was erected in the exact specifications that God had commanded many years previously. Within the Temple was a large and heavy curtain that signified the separation of God from the people because of their sin. Beyond the curtain was the Holy of Holies. Once a year, on the Day of Atonement, the high priest from the tribe of Levi entered the Holy of Holies and sprinkled the blood of a slain lamb on the altar of God, known as the Ark of the Covenant. The people would know that the innocent animal had died exclusively because of their sins, and it was through this blood sacrifice that their sins were forgiven. God in His mercy had granted a way for His people to atone for their sins and come into His presence.

As magnificent as this Temple was, it was merely a dim reflection of the permanent temple God would someday provide. After all, the Temple was built by man and could be destroyed, which it was several times during the course of Israel's history. And the sacrifice for atonement would have to be made repeatedly year after year. God planned for a future forever temple and a permanent sacrifice.

The enmity that God had ordained in Genesis between Satan and the offspring of Eve was apparent. Satan continued to tempt individuals into sin throughout the history of Israel. It was always God's desire that man and woman would stand strong and choose to obey Him out of love rather than to yield to the lies of Satan.

The book of JOB records one man's faith in the midst of Satan's attacks. While it's uncertain when during the history of Israel Job lived, he was a model of one who would hold true to God's commands, despite Satan's temptations. Satan took Job's property, took Job's children, inflicted Job with pain and illness. Yet despite all Satan did, he couldn't break Job's faith. Job's story is a picture of God's power over Satan. Job also prophetically looked forward to a time when the Savior would come. He declared: "For I know that my redeemer lives, and at the last he will stand upon the earth. And after my skin has been thus destroyed, yet in my flesh I shall see God" (Job 19:25–26). Job was a descendant of Abraham who witnessed and testified that God's blessings were to be eternal—there remained a promise that a redeemer would conquer death.

Personal Application

Do you consider yourself a wise person? Why or why not?

Where do you tend to go for wisdom?

James 1:5 says, "If any of you lacks wisdom, let him ask God, who gives generously to all without reproach, and it will be given him." What circumstances or struggles in your life right now need a dose of God's wisdom? How does the truth that "it will be given" encourage you?

Recall a time of suffering in your own life. Did your circumstances change your relationship with God? If so, in what way? How might wisdom have influenced your response?

Read Isaiah 43:2-3 below.

"When you pass through the waters, I will be with you;
and through the rivers, they shall not overwhelm you;
when you walk through fire you shall not be burned,
and the flame shall not consume you.
For I am the Lord your God,
the Holy One of Israel, your Savior.
I give Egypt as your ransom,
Cush and Seba in exchange for you."

What truths can you cling to during times of trials or suffering? (For additional insight see Romans 8:28, Hebrews 13:5b-6)

How would you answer the question, "Why does God allow suffering?"

[Author's Note: If you struggle with the question above, see the following verses for more insight on the purpose of suffering: 2 Corinthians 12:7-10, 1 Peter 1:6-7, Romans 5:3-5, 2 Corinthians 1:3-4.]

After the loss of his children and his possessions, Job proclaimed, "The Lord gave, and the Lord has taken away. Blessed be the name of the Lord" (1:21b). How do you think it was possible for Job to say these words and maintain his faith despite his circumstances?

In the midst of hurting and loss, do you believe that God is still worthy of praise?

Additional Notes:

WEEK 16:
The Divided Kingdom

"The days of punishment have come; the days of recompense have come; Israel shall know it."

—HOSEA 9:7A

Scripture: Selected passages from 1st and 2nd Kings, 1st and 2nd Chronicles, Amos and Hosea

[Author's Note: There were twelve tribes of Israel, who were descendants of the twelve sons of Jacob. All but one (the priestly tribe of Levi) were allotted land. Joseph was allotted two portions through his two sons. It was God's will that they form one nation under His Kingship. At this point in HIStory, they had been given a human king to rule. Throughout the history of the tribes there had been conflict among the tribes. Details about the conflict can be found in passages such as Judges 20 and 2 Samuel 2–3. The conflict did not please God, and the consequences for their disobedience will be examined in this week's lesson.]

1. Read 1 Kings 11:26–40. What did the prophet, Ahijah, tell Jeroboam that God was going to give him?

   How was God going to keep His promise to David?

2. How was this prophecy fulfilled? See 1 Kings 12:1–24.

3. What tribes became part of the southern kingdom (known as Judah) and who became their king? Who became the king of the northern kingdom, known as Israel?

Southern kingdom (Judah) → King: _____

Tribes: _____

Northern kingdom (Israel) → King: _____

Tribes: _____

The history of Israel, the northern kingdom:

4. What sins did Jeroboam commit? See 1 Kings 12:25-33. (For additional context reference Exodus 20:4-5.)

How did Jeroboam create a man-made religion? See 2 Chronicles 11:13-15.

5. Below is a list of all the kings of the northern kingdom of Israel. Look up two or three of the passages. What did all of the kings have in common?

Is there a particular phrase that is repeated when describing their reign? What does this phrase mean?

THE KINGS OF THE NORTHERN KINGDOM OF ISRAEL:		
Jeroboam	1 Kings 12:25-14:20	931-910 BC
Nadab	1 Kings 15:25-28	910-909 BC
Baasha	1 Kings 15:33-16:7	909-886 BC
Elah	1 Kings 16:8-10	886-885 BC
Zimri	1 Kings 16:10-20	885 BC
Omri	1 Kings 16:21-28	885-874 BC
Ahab	1 Kings 16:29-22:40	874-853 BC
Ahaziah	1 Kings 22:51-53	853-852 BC

THE KINGS OF THE NORTHERN KINGDOM OF ISRAEL:		
Jehoram/Joram	2 Kings 2:19–8:15	852–841 BC
Jehu	2 Kings 9:1–10:35	841–814 BC
Jehoahaz	2 Kings 13:1–9	814–798 BC
Jehoash	2 Kings 13:10–25	798–782 BC
Jeroboam II	2 Kings 14:23–29	793–753 BC
Zechariah	2 Kings 15:8–12	753 BC
Shallum	2 Kings 15:13–16	752 BC
Menahem	2 Kings 15:17–22	752–742 BC
Pekahiah	2 Kings 15:23–26	742–740 BC
Pekah	2 Kings 15:27–31	740–732 BC
Hoshea	2 Kings 17:1–6	732–722 BC

The Prophet Elijah:

6. Read 1 Kings 18:15–40. Who did God send to warn the nation to turn from its wickedness? What did the prophet do afterwards?

What do you learn about prayer from this prophet?

7. What do we learn about the prophets of Baal from this account?

8.   What do you learn about God's power in 2 Kings 1:9-12?

9.   9.   Ahab and the people of Israel were trying to serve both the pagan gods and the Lord God (Yahweh). What does Yahweh say about serving Him and only Him? (For additional insight see Ex. 20:2-3.)

The Prophet Amos:

10.   For what iniquities of Israel does the prophet Amos declare God's judgment? See Amos 2:6-8. (You may want to read in several translations to see the iniquities clearly.) Do you still see these sins still today? What does that tell you about mankind?

11.   Of what does Amos remind the people in verse 3:2a? (For the best understanding of this verse, you may want to read the passage in a few different translations.)

[Author's Note: As HIStory unfolds we will see that the Lord has selected us—the Church—to be His "chosen race, a royal priesthood, a holy nation, a people for his own possession, that you may proclaim the excellencies of him who called you out of darkness into his marvelous light." (1 Peter 2:9).]

12.   Read Amos 7:7-9. What is a "plumb line"?

What does having a "plumb line" say about what God was doing among His people?

The Prophet Hosea:

13. The prophet, Hosea, compared the unfaithfulness of Israel to that of an adulterous marriage relationship. How is that an apt metaphor?

14. Read Hosea 3. What did God tell Hosea to do and why?

What does this passage teach us about God's goodness, love and forgiveness?

15. What is the core of Israel's disobedience? See Hosea 4:1, 6, 14.

   a. Using a dictionary, define the word "knowledge."

   b. What knowledge did the people lack? How can this knowledge be attained?

16. How did what Israel give to the Lord, differ from what God desired from them? See Hosea 6:6.

17. What warnings to Israel do you find in these passages in Amos 5:27 and Hosea 11:5? (For additional insight see Deuteronomy 28:15, 36 and 1 Kings 14:15-16.)

18. What ultimately happened to the northern kingdom and why? (HIStory records that this happened in 722 BC). Read 2 Kings 17:6-17. How were God's prophetic warnings fulfilled?

19. Read Amos 9:11-15. What hope does God promise to the Israelites?

SUMMARY WEEK 16

HIStory Continues...

Each of the twelve tribes, which made up God's chosen nation, had descended from the sons of Israel (Jacob). Just as with squabbling children, the tribes often argued among themselves. God wanted them to be unified as one nation under His Kingship, but because of their continued disobedience to Him, the nation of Israel would one day divide. He foretold this through His prophet Ahijah.

In a display of God's sovereignty, the nations did divide after Solomon's death. Just as prophesied, a servant of Solomon, Jeroboam, was given authority to rule over ten of the northern tribes. Solomon's son, Rehoboam, became king over the southern two tribes of Judah and Benjamin. The northern ten tribes became the nation of Israel. The two southern tribes became known as the nation of Judah. They were all God's chosen people, but sadly divided. The history of the divided kingdom of Israel is recounted in I and II KINGS and I and II CHRONICLES.

Under the leadership of many evil kings, both nations often worshiped idols and took on the pagan practices of the nations that surrounded them. The Temple was no longer the exclusive place of worship for God's people. Despite the continued disobedience, God warned them to return to Him. His grace was abundant, and He called them to repent time and time again through His spokesmen, the Major and Minor Prophets.

The prophets gave warnings of future judgment for disobedience as well as hope for redemption. The essential message to Israel and Judah was that they weren't to rely on their own strength, nor were they to make allies with the neighboring pagan nations. This had been the same message Moses had given to the people upon entering the Promised Land. God wasn't discriminating. This was to protect His people. The surrounding nations were evil, and God's eternal warning would be to reject the evil practices and idols of this world. God knew that if His people didn't separate themselves from the world, they'd become like the pagan nations rather than like God.

The prophets also foretold of three different future periods: (1) a near future time of captivity if the nations didn't repent, (2) a more distant future when the Savior would come to save them from their sins, (3) and a far future time when the Savior would return to establish His eternal Kingdom. The words of the prophets can be divided into the following categories: prophets to Israel (the northern kingdom), prophets to the surrounding nations, prophets to Judah (the southern kingdom) prior to exile into Babylon, prophets to Judah during their exile, and prophets to Judah after being released from exile.

The prophets Elijah and Elisha were faithful spokesmen of God who called the northern kingdom of Israel to turn their hearts to Him. Other prophets to Israel, with books named after them, spoke warnings of judgment.

AMOS condemned not only Israel's neighbors, but also Israel itself for violating God's laws. He warned the people that if they continued with the practice of idolatry and sinfulness, they'd be taken captive by the powerful and evil nation of Assyria.

HOSEA was the last of the prophets who spoke to the northern kingdom of Israel. While the other prophets emphasized power and justice as the essential characteristics of God, Hosea gave a picture of God's forgiveness for unfaithfulness. God would never forsake them, even if He allowed punishment.

Sadly, Israel didn't respect God's warnings, so as foretold, the nation of Assyria succeeded in taking Israel captive in 722 bc (2 Kings 17). The northern kingdom of Israel ceased and its people, who represented ten of the twelve tribes, were scattered outside the Promised Land. If God had promised that the Savior would come from one of the northern tribes, the fulfillment of His promise would have been impossible to verify. God, however, had promised He would come from the tribe of Judah, part of the southern kingdom.

Personal Application

This week we see God discipline His children. Have you ever experienced God's discipline in your life? If so, when and how?

How is discipline ultimately a loving action?

Likewise, how have you experienced God's restoration from brokenness or sin?

How do you think God can be loving, but have a steady opposition to sin? What does this tell you about His character? How is His opposition to sin encouraging?

★ **For a Deeper Dive:** In the Old Testament, the law was God's plumb line. The history of the Israelites demonstrates that no one on their own can be "plumb" with God as the holy standard. How does this truth demonstrate mankind's need for a Savior?

Write down any additional insights or things you learned this week:

Additional Notes:

WEEK 17:
Prophets to Nations

"Now the word of the Lord came to Jonah the son of Amittai, saying, "Arise, go to Nineveh, that great city, and call out against it, for their evil has come up before me." But Jonah rose to flee to Tarshish from the presence of the Lord. He went down to Joppa and found a ship going to Tarshish. So he paid the fare and went down into it, to go with them to Tarshish, away from the presence of the Lord."

– J O N A H   1 : 1 - 3

Scripture: Selected passages in Obadiah, Jonah, and Nahum

The Prophet Jonah

Scripture: Read the entire book of Jonah.

1. What did God ask Jonah to do? What does his request reveal about God?

[Author's Note: Jonah prophesied before the northern kingdom of Israel was taken into captivity by Assyria. Assyria, (including its capital of Nineveh) was in temporary decline during the reign of Jeroboam. We can only speculate as to whether Jonah would have known of the prophecies of Amos and Hosea, who had foretold of the eventual captivity and demise of the northern kingdom.]

2. What did Jonah do? What does it mean that Jonah went "away from the presence of the Lord"?

Read Psalm 139:7. Is it possible to run from God completely?

3. What was Jonah's reason for not wanting to preach to Nineveh? See Jonah 4:2.

4. What did God do to change Jonah's plans?

    What does this reveal about God?

5. Closely examine Jonah's prayer in chapter 2. List all the things that Jonah knows about God.

6. The prophet, Nahum, would also preach to Nineveh at a later time. Identify the sins of Nineveh from Nahum 3:1-4.

7. God gave Jonah a second chance to obey. What was the message that Jonah gave to the Ninevites? How did the people of Nineveh respond? (For further insight as to what it meant to put on sackcloth as in the case of Nineveh, see Daniel 9:3-6.)

8. What does it mean to repent? Use a dictionary or concordance.

9. What was God's response to the pleas of the pagan people of Nineveh?

10. What does the story of Jonah teach about God's mercy, even to pagan nations?

11. ★ **For a Deeper Dive:** What do you learn about God's mercy from the following passages?

    a. Jeremiah 18:7-10

    b. Romans 5:6-8

12. In your own words, define mercy.

13. What is Jonah's response to God in chapter 4? Is his emotion justified?

    What does Jonah's response reveal about his heart?

    How does Jonah's heart compare with the heart of God?

14. What illustration does God show Jonah to change his heart? Describe it below.

The Prophet Obadiah

Scripture: Read the entire book of Obadiah. (It is very short!)

[Author's Note: Obadiah was a prophet called to warn the foreign nation of Edom of God's judgment. It is uncertain at what point in HIStory he prophesied. The questions regarding this book of Scripture are included here because they further explore God's mercy to nations other than Israel.]

15. The nation of Edom was formed by the the descendants of Esau, the brother of Jacob/Israel. What do you learn about the relationship between Edom and Israel from Obadiah 1:10? (For additional insight, see Numbers 20:14-21; Judges 11:17-18; Psalm 83:1-6.)

16. What was the root of Edom's sin as noted in Obadiah 1:3? How did this sin lead to other sins by the nation of Edom?

17. ★ **For a Deeper Dive:** Take some time to research online or in other resources the following: What happened to Nineveh and Edom? How were the prophecies fulfilled?

    What does this tell us about how God will protect and defend His people?

SUMMARY WEEK 17

HIStory Continues...

God warned the surrounding nations that there would be destruction if they were evil and brought harm to His people. He would hold the nations accountable, but He gave them opportunities to do what was right in His sight. Further, when His promises came true and were recorded in history, this would be evidence that God was the one true God. God demonstrated His sovereignty and His control of the destinies of every nation. We see in the words of the prophets that God didn't just come to save the Israelites, but the blessings were meant for all. Somehow, the promised Savior would bless everyone who received Him.

OBADIAH was sent to the nation of Edom (descendants of Esau). He foretold that their pride and cruelty against Israel would be their downfall.

God asked JONAH to preach to the evil Ninevites. However, Jonah was an Israelite and didn't like the idea that God was offering these evildoers, who had committed atrocities to his fellow people, a chance to repent. Jonah didn't want to offer them mercy. He wanted the people of Nineveh to be destroyed. Because of his disobedience to God, Jonah found himself thrown into the sea where he was swallowed by a great fish. Jonah called to God in his distress, and God rescued him after three days and three nights. Jonah was given a second chance to obey and he did. He went into Nineveh and preached of God's plan to overthrow the city if they didn't turn from their evil ways. The king and the people of Nineveh repented. God abandoned the disaster set to befall them. Jonah had done what God asked of him, but he was still angry with God for showing mercy to the Ninevites. But God demonstrated to Jonah that He pities those who don't know Him and wants to give all an opportunity to repent.

God in his mercy had spared this nation once after Jonah's warning, but it continued its practice of evil. Nahum the prophet was also sent to Nineveh with the message that God is slow to display His wrath, but that He avenges sin and unrighteousness. Nineveh is the capital of Assyria. The cruelty of Assyria is documented in the book of NAHUM, as well as in history. It's referred to as "the city of blood," with "many casualties, piles of dead, bodies without number, people stumbling over the corpses" (Nahum 3). The practices of the Assyrians were cruel. They skinned men alive, removed their tongues, and dismembered their bodies. The evil they inflicted on His people finally resulted in God's display of judgment.

God, through the prophets, made predictions regarding the surrounding nations if they didn't repent. It all came true just as he said. The history books record this.

Personal Application

★ **For a Deeper Dive:** When the Promised Savior comes in the flesh, He gives a "commission" to His followers. For a look ahead, read Matthew 28:19-20. How is the New Testament commission similar to what God asked Jonah to do?

What is God calling you to do to build His Kingdom here on earth?

Name a time that you have been called by God to share HIStory (or something about God) with someone. How did you respond?

Have you ever felt called to share with someone that you felt was beyond receiving the mercy of God? Have you ever not shared with someone just because you felt that they wouldn't respond in obedience to God? If so, when?

How may the story of Jonah prompt you to share more boldly and faithfully?

Has there been or is there anyone in your life that you have been angry with, but you should instead extend mercy? Is there anyone in your life that you need to give a "second chance" like God gave to Jonah?

Often times, showing mercy can be seen as being "weak." Do you agree or disagree? Why or why not?

Additional Notes:

WEEK 18:
Prophet Isaiah Called

"Of the increase of his government and of peace there will be no end, on the throne of David and over his kingdom, to establish it and to uphold it with justice and with righteousness from this time forth and forevermore. The zeal of the Lord of hosts will do this."

- I S A I A H   9 : 7

Scripture: Selected passages from Isaiah, 2 Kings

[Author's Note: Isaiah's name means "salvation of the Lord" or "the Lord is salvation." Salvation is actually one of the major themes of his message, and the word salvation occurs over twenty times in the book bearing his name. Isaiah prophesied during the reigns of Uzziah, Jotham, Ahaz and Hezekiah. These were kings of the southern kingdom of Judah, and Isaiah's message is mainly directed toward the southern kingdom of Judah. Keep in mind God's promise that the Savior would come from the line of David, the tribe of Judah, which is the southern kingdom of Israel.]

1. Consider what the word "salvation" means. How have you seen this attribute of God thus far in HIStory?

2. The reign of King Uzziah is described in 2 Chronicles 26. How did Uzziah begin his reign? (See 2 Chronicles 26:1-5)

   How did he end his reign? (See 2 Chronicles 26:16-21.) What was the cause of his demise?

   At this point in HIStory we have seen many struggle with this sin. Many theologians say this sin is the root cause of all sin. Do you agree or disagree?

3. Read Isaiah 6. What do you learn about the Promised King?

In light of what you have just learned about the end of Uzziah's reign and his moral condition, how does he contrast with the King whom Isaiah saw?

4. How would you define the word, "holy"? Use a Bible dictionary or concordance if necessary.

5. What did Isaiah notice about himself and the people of Judah when he saw the Lord? See also Isaiah 64:6.

6. How was Isaiah's sin atoned for as noted in Isaiah 6?

What does this action tell us about how we are to come into God's presence?

Isaiah's prophecies cover a large expanse of time. The following Scriptures will give you an overview of the history:

The Assyrian Threat

a. What happened to the northern kingdom at the hands of the Assyrians? Why? See 2 Kings 17:6–18.

b. What happened to the southern kingdom? Why? (Hezekiah was the king of Judah, the southern kingdom.) See 2 Kings 19:14-38.

c. What was Judah called to do in order to avoid judgment for its many sins? See Isaiah 1:16-20.

d. What ultimately happened to Assyria? See 2 Kings 19:32-37.

The Babylonian Threat

a. What was the warning that Isaiah gave to Judah? See Isaiah 39:5-7.

b. [Author's Note: The southern kingdom was carried off into exile in several separate events and recorded in 2 Kings 24-25 and Jeremiah 52.]

Read 2 Kings 25:8-9. What happened to the house of the Lord?

c. Read Isaiah 45:1. Who specifically does Isaiah prophesy will save the nation of Judah?

d. How was this prophecy fulfilled? See 2 Chronicles 36:22-23 and Ezra 1:1-4.

e. ★ **For a Deeper Dive:** Conservative Christian scholars have dated Isaiah's writings from 701-681 B.C. Considering that historical records date Cyrus' reign in the 500's B.C., how can one explain the prophecy, but for God's inspiration? Isaiah's prophecy was made before Cyrus was born!

7. ★ **For a Deeper Dive:** Isaiah gives more references to the coming Savior than any other prophet. Examine the following prophetic words. What do these verses tell you about the coming Savior?

SCRIPTURE	PROPHECY
Isaiah 11:1	
Isaiah 7:14	
Isaiah 8:8, 10	
Isaiah 8:14	
Isaiah 9:6	
Isaiah 11:2	
Isaiah 26:19	
Isaiah 28:16	
Isaiah 59:20	

8. Isaiah 52:14–53:12 is one of the most important prophecies regarding the coming Savior and our promised salvation. List below everything you learn about Him and His mission.

9. Isaiah, as well as other prophets, also referred to a second coming of the Savior, in other words a far-in-the-future fulfillment of the prophecies. (Remember that prophecy often had dual and at times triple fulfillment. Prophetic messages spoke of events that would be fulfilled in Israel's near future, the distant future, and the far in the distant future. They took an extended series of events and collapsed them so that the near and distant events could appear to be only one event.) What do you learn from the following verses:

    a. Isaiah 2:2-4

    b. Isaiah 9:7

    c. Isaiah 40:10-11

10. From your study of the prophets thus far, what reasons could God have had for sending them and His Word to the people?

11. Isaiah painted a picture of evil in the world. Fortunately God's message doesn't end in doom. What future hope does he also provide? See Isaiah 65:17-25.

SUMMARY WEEK 18

HIStory Continues...

The ten tribes living in the northern kingdom had been conquered. God's promise of a Savior coming from the lineage of Abraham would now have to be fulfilled through the descendants in the southern kingdom. There were only two tribes in the southern kingdom—Benjamin and Judah. God had earlier promised that the Savior would come from the tribe of Judah.

Kings ruled Judah at this time. The idea of worldly kings to govern the people was not God's perfect plan for them. Kings of the world couldn't be trusted. When these kings did evil in the eyes of the Lord, the people would stray and follow their earthly kings. God sent prophets to Judah in the southern kingdom to warn them to obey God. God wanted his people to turn to Him, to let Him alone rule their lives and nation.

Judah did have some obedient kings among those who ruled her who attempted to destroy idolatry and restore the worship God had commanded. When Assyria tried to overthrow Judah, God spared her because of the righteousness of King Hezekiah and the influence of prominent prophets. But His people were still sinful and there were consequences for her sin.

ISAIAH warned of Judah's captivity by the evil empire of Babylon if Judah didn't obey. He also prophesied that a man named Cyrus would subdue Babylon and let God's people be freed without any ransom paid. Isaiah made this prophecy 150 years before a Persian king named Cyrus was born.

The prophecies of Isaiah extended beyond the near future of God's people. More than any other prophet, Isaiah prophesied about the coming Savior and His Kingdom. The promise of Abraham was to be preserved. God, through Isaiah, gave greater indicators of how the Savior would be identified. For example, Isaiah said the Messiah would be born to a virgin and preceded by one who would call all to repentance.

Isaiah also gave specifics of how the Messiah would save. He would be a sacrifice, a suffering servant, who would redeem the people. He would be pierced for our sins (our transgressions). He would be mocked and flogged. He would suffer as He saved.

Isaiah described a Savior who would be more than a political or military conqueror. The Savior's mission would be for the purpose God set forth from the beginning, to reconcile man and woman with God. He—the Savior and Messiah—would take upon Himself our iniquities, and He would receive the punishment on our behalf for our sins. He could only do this if He were Himself without sin. Isaiah makes clear that the coming Savior would be a sinless man who would suffer for the sake of the world.

Isaiah also looked forward to an eternal reign of the coming Savior: "For to us a child is born, to us a son is given; and the government shall be upon his shoulder, and his name shall be called Wonderful Counselor, Mighty God, Everlasting Father, Prince of Peace. Of the increase of his government and of peace there will be no end, on the throne of David and over his kingdom, to establish it and to uphold it with justice and with righteousness from this time forth and forevermore. The zeal of the Lord of hosts will do this" (Isaiah 9:6–7).

This passage illustrates that Isaiah looked forward to an everlasting reign of peace. But doesn't the history of the world tell us that peace is not possible with mere mortals in charge? We're called to combat evil. Our success, however, can only be limited because of the greed and hard hearts of political rulers, dictators, and terrorists throughout the world. So how could Isaiah boldly proclaim with confidence that one day there would be everlasting peace?

The peace that Isaiah foresaw would be ushered in by a different kind of king. After all, how could a mere mortal man reign forever? Isaiah's prophecy clearly stated that He would be human: "For to us a child is born..." However, in order to reign forever, He would have to be more than human. He would be Mighty God, Everlasting Father, and Prince of Peace! The coming Savior would come to us fully human and yet fully God. Only that kind of king could lead the world to peace. This knowledge gave Isaiah the boldness to profess truth to the world in face of evil.

Personal Application

Isaiah 6:3 says, "Holy, holy, holy is the Lord." Describe the magnitude of God's holiness in your own words.

Why does His holiness matter?

Does the depravity and evil in the world ever upset you? Name a few instances that upset you the most.

Why has there never been world-wide peace?

Consider Isaiah's response before God in Isaiah 6:5, "Woe is me! For I am lost; for I am a man of unclean lips, and I dwell in the midst of a people of unclean lips; for my eyes have seen the King, the Lord of hosts!" What does Isaiah's words tell you about his own recognition of his "status" before God?

If you were standing before the Lord, what words would you say to acknowledge your unholiness? Write them below.

With regards to the Promised Savior Isaiah prophesies, "Of the increase of his government and of peace there will be no end" (9:7). How does the promise of everlasting peace through the Savior bring you encouragement?

Additional Notes:

WEEK 19:
Daniel Among Prophets

"When Daniel knew that the document had been signed, he went to his house where he had windows in his upper chamber open toward Jerusalem. He got down on his knees three times a day and prayed and gave thanks before his God, as he had done previously."

– DANIEL 6:10

Scripture: Selected passages from Micah, Zephaniah, Jeremiah, Lamentations, Habakkuk and Daniel.

Scripture: Micah

1. The themes that we saw in Isaiah are repeated in Micah:

   a. Micah identified the sins of the capital cities of Samaria (the northern kingdom) and Jerusalem (the southern kingdom)

   b. Micah warned of destruction for their disobedience

   c. Micah spoke of restoration of Jerusalem and the future hope of a Savior

   How do you see these themes in the following passages:

   Micah 1:1-9

   Micah 4:6-7

   Micah 5:2

   What more do we learn about the Promised Savior from Micah 5:2?

2.   Spend some time reflecting on Micah 6:8. In your own words, what does it mean to:

   a.   Do justice

   b.   Love kindness

   c.   Walk humbly with your God

Scripture: Zephaniah

   [Author's Note: Zephaniah was another prophet who warned the southern kingdom of their coming judgment. He is also known for his prophesies regarding far-in-the-future events which are examined below.]

3.   What future event does Zephaniah 1:7, 14 refer to? (For additional insight see Isaiah 2:12; 13:6,9; Ezekiel 13:5; 30:3; Joel 1:15; Amos 5:18, 20; Obadiah 15; Zechariah 14:1; Malachi 4:5.)

   ★ **For a Deeper Dive:** See the New Testament references in Acts 2:20-21; 1 Thessalonians 5:2; 2 Thessalonians 2:2; 2 Peter 3:10; Revelation 6:17; 16:14. What additional information do these verses give you about "the day of the Lord"?

Scripture: Jeremiah and Lamentations

[Author's Note: Jeremiah was another prophet during the decline of Judah, and the Babylonian rise to power. He began his ministry during the reign of the last faithful king of the southern kingdom. During his life the people went into exile and the Temple was destroyed.]

4. What significant event is recorded in 2 Kings 22? What was was King Josiah's reaction? How was he rewarded by God? (See verses 18-20.)

5. Jeremiah, like the other prophets, identified the sins and evil practices of the people. What consequence did Jeremiah preach? (See Jeremiah 16:5-13; 26:4-6.)

    How is this is consistent with God's love?

    Is it possible to reconcile God's attributes of justice and mercy? See Romans 2:4-11; 2 Peter 3:9 for more insight.

6. How was Jeremiah's message received? See Jeremiah 12:6; 20:1-2; 26:7-11.

7. Jeremiah was able to prophesy boldly in the face of death. How was he able to stand strong? Consider Jeremiah 1:4-10 and Lamentations 3:23-24.

8. ★ **For a Deeper Dive:** What promise of hope and dual fulfillment is prophesied in Jeremiah 23:1-8 and 29:10-14? How does this confirm the covenant made with Abraham and renewed to David?

9. **BONUS DEEP DIVE:** Read Jeremiah 31:31-34. What does God promise? Read ahead in HIStory in Hebrews 8:8-13.

Scripture: Daniel

10. Read Daniel chapter 1 in its entirety.

    What happened to Daniel, Shadrach, Meshach and Abednego?

    How did they determine to honor the God of Israel?

    How did God bless them?

11. Daniel 2 recounts the story of the Babylonian (Chaldean) king, Nebuchadnezzar. He was troubled by dreams and ordered that the magicians under his kingdom interpret the dreams in order to settle his spirit. None of them could, and he commanded that all the wise men of Babylon be destroyed. Read Daniel 2:17-49.

    What did Daniel know about God, and how did God equip him?

How was Daniel rewarded by Nebuchadnezzar?

12. Read Daniel 3–4:3, the historical account of Nebuchadnezzar's golden image. What did the king command people to do?

What was the consequence for not obeying Nebuchadnezzar stated in 3:6?

13. How do the three Jewish men respond to the charge against them in 3:16–18?

What does the phrase "but if not" (verse 18) tell you about their belief in God's sovereignty over their circumstance?

14. Read Daniel 6. What specific descriptions of Daniel and his faith can you identify in these verses?

What does King Darius observe about Daniel's faith in 9:16, 20?

15. Daniel 6:22-23 says, "My God sent his angel and shut the lions' mouths, and they have not harmed me, because I was found blameless before him; and also before you, O king, I have done no harm." Then the king was exceedingly glad, and commanded that Daniel be taken up out of the den. So Daniel was taken up out of the den, and no kind of harm was found on him, because he had trusted in his God."

Who does Daniel credit for his safety?

[Author's Note: While the book of Daniel is included as one of the historical books of the Old Testament, it is also one of the most important prophetic books. Specifically, Daniel's prophecies regarding the "Day of the Lord" or last days, and Daniel's apocalyptic visions are meant to give hope of the Savior's ultimate victory over evil. A study of these visions are beyond the scope of this study, but would be the subject of a wonderful indepth study.]

★ **For a Deeper Dive:** See Daniel 12 and a far-in-the-future look ahead at the end times and the final battle with evil. What hope for believers can you identify?

SUMMARY WEEK 19

HIStory continues...

MICAH was another prophet to the southern kingdom of Judah. He further narrowed the identity of the coming Messiah. He prophesied the Savior would come from Bethlehem.

ZEPHANIAH foretold the destruction and restoration of the capital city of Jerusalem.

JEREMIAH prophesied boldly for forty years trying to avert the Babylonian captivity. He told Judah they would be deported to Babylon as slaves for seventy years. God had delivered His people to a bountiful country and was indeed upset with them. One day, when the Savior came, the Law of God would no longer be a list of do's and don'ts. They would follow God with their hearts. Jeremiah spoke of a new covenant that God would have with His people.

"Behold, the days are coming, declares the Lord, when I will make a new covenant with the house of Israel and the house of Judah, not like the covenant that I made with their fathers on the day when I took them by the hand to bring them out of the land of Egypt, my covenant that they broke, though I was their husband, declares the Lord. For this is the covenant that I will make with the house of Israel after those days, declares the Lord: I will put my law within them, and I will write it on their hearts. And I will be their God, and they shall be my people. And no longer shall each one teach his neighbor and each his brother, saying, 'Know the Lord,' for they shall all know me, from the least of them to the greatest, declares the Lord. For I will forgive their iniquity, and I will remember their sin no more" (Jeremiah 31:31–34).

In the book called LAMENTATIONS, Jeremiah wrote a poem. It was full of weeping and lamenting the fall of Jerusalem and the affliction of his people, which God had allowed as judgment for its disobedience.

HABAKKUK cried to God because of the wickedness of Judah. God assured him that His judgment was coming on Judah.

And finally, the prophecies of Isaiah and the other prophets came to pass. Sadly, the Temple was destroyed, the people were captured, and they were sent to exile in Babylon. God had told the Israelites the consequences for disobedience. God had to enforce those consequences. His justice would require nothing less. The Israelites had chosen disobedience. God had been very specific in His timeline and history records that the captivity lasted seventy years, exactly as was prophesied.

God sent more prophets to the people while they were in exile to comfort and reassure them that they would return to their homeland. He had to punish them, but He didn't leave them alone without His word and His hope.

DANIEL prophesied of God's protection, the restoration of His people to their land, and the promise of the future Messianic Kingdom. He gave a message of hope that some of God's people would survive. Not only did he also confirm that the time of captivity would be seventy years, but he also prophesied as to the timing of the coming of the Messiah and foretold events far in the future—specifically a second coming of the Messiah when He would be given glory and dominion over all nations. Daniel spoke of an everlasting Kingdom. Daniel, like other Old Testament figures such as Joseph and David, also gave a picture of the Savior.

Daniel's life was an example of how it's possible to faithfully obey God despite oppression. As a young man, Daniel was taken into captivity and through obedience and hard work he became an administrator in the pagan nation. There he was tempted to renounce his faith by agreeing not to pray to God and thus avoid being thrown into the lion's den. But Daniel refused to give up his habit of prayer. The king, though he favored Daniel, was forced to carry out the punishment. A merciful God closed the mouths of the lions and Daniel was spared death. Daniel, by his faithfulness in trials, was a foreshadowing of the promised Savior.

Personal Application

Daniel, Shadrach, Meshach and Abednego were all living in exile in a pagan nation, yet they refused to compromise their beliefs (and trust) in their God. In what ways does the current culture challenge your beliefs?

How can you replicate their steadfastness and not compromise your beliefs?

Despite facing the fiery furnace, Shadrach, Meshach and Abednego declare that their "God is able to deliver" them (Daniel 3:16-18). Likewise, Daniel was kept safe in the lion's den, "because he had trusted in his God" (9:23b). How do you think these men cultivated this kind of trust in God and his power?

What does trusting God in fiery trails look like in your life?

Daniel 6:10 says he got "down on his knees three times a day and prayed and gave thanks before his God, as he had done previously." What does this tell you about the importance (and frequency) of prayer?

What does your prayer life look like? How can you be more intentional with your prayers?

Reread the prayer of Habakkuk:

"Though the fig tree should not blossom, nor fruit be on the vines, the produce of the olive fail and the fields yield no food, the flock be cut off from the fold and there be no herd in the stalls, yet I will rejoice in the Lord; I will take joy in the God of my salvation. God, the Lord, is my strength; he makes my feet like the deer's; he makes me tread on my high places." –Habakkuk 3:17–19

Write your own prayer to the Lord modeled after this prayer.

Additional Notes:

WEEK 20:
The Final Prophets

"Behold, I send my messenger, and he will prepare the way before me. And the Lord whom you seek will suddenly come to His temple; and the messenger of the covenant in whom you delight, behold, he is coming, says the Lord of hosts."

- MALACHI 3:1

Scripture: Selected passages from 2 Chronicles, Ezekiel, Esther, Joel, Ezra, Nehemiah, Haggai, Zechariah and Malachi.

For a brief review of the history regarding Judah from the time of its last kings until its exile, read 2 Chronicles 36:17-21. You may find it helpful to summarize the history of the southern kingdom, and record how the words of the prophets were fulfilled.

The Prophet Ezekiel [A prophet during the exile of the Judeans in Babylon]

1. The Lord, through Ezekiel, reminded the people of the purpose of His discipline. What reason did He give? See Ezekiel 7:9. (For additional insight see Ezekiel 3:9; 20:20, 44; 23:49; 24:24; 28:22, 24, 26; 29:26; 34:30; 36:23; 39:22, 28.)

   What does this tell you about God's purpose for the Israelites and for us?

2. Where before in HIStory have you seen this phrase repeated in Scripture? (See Exodus 10:2; 14:4; 14:18). What does this also tell you about the Israelites inability to follow the Law, and the condition of the human heart?

3. ⭐ **For a Deeper Dive:** Read ahead in Romans 3:9-20. What does God, through the prophet Ezekiel, promise? See also Ezekiel 36:27-28.

4. Read Ezekiel 34 in its entirety. Describe the leaders of Israel (the shepherds):

Who are the sheep? How have the sheep been adversely affected by their shepherds?

What promises does God make regarding the sheep? See Ezekiel 34:25-31.

★ **For a Deeper Dive:** Once again, there is a promise of a future, dual fulfillment. What more do we learn about the Promised Savior from Ezekiel?

Post-Exilic history: [Author's Note: After 70 years of captivity (exactly as prophesied), the Babylonian empire was conquered by the Persian empire. King Cyrus of Persia allowed the Israelites to return to their homeland in 538 B.C., and God sent prophets to the people to encourage them to return to Jerusalem and build the temple that had been destroyed. This week we will see some of the post-exilic messages of warning and promise. The people to whom the prophets spoke would not experience the former glories of Israel, nor would they see all of the promises fulfilled. Their prophets heralded a future fulfillment—a new covenant, and new era with the coming of the promised Savior and Hero. Hallelujah!]

The Prophet Ezra:

5. Read 2 Chronicles 36:22-23 and Ezra 1. What was the king's edict? How and why did it come about?

6. Why was the rebuilding of the Temple important to God? How were the materials provided? How did this fulfil the prophecy of Jeremiah 27:21-22?

7. Ezra 4 records that there were adversaries who were opposed to the rebuilding of the Temple? Why wouldn't the Jewish leaders allow them to help?

The adversaries used various means to halt the building of the temple and later the wall around Jerusalem. What were their ploys?

The Prophets Haggai & Zechariah:

8. Read Haggai chapter 2:7-9. What else do you learn about the importance of the Temple, and what it represented?

9. Nearly 20 years after the return from exile into Babylon, the Temple was still not completed. Enemies of Israel continued to oppress the people, and they fell into disobedience. Both Haggai and Zechariah moved the people to complete the Temple. Zechariah encouraged the people with visions of the future. What more does he tell us about the coming Savior? See Zechariah 9:9.

The Prophet Nehemiah:

10. Nehemiah was responsible for the rebuilding of the wall in Jerusalem which would help protect the Temple. Not only did Nehemiah help restore the physical aspects of the Temple and the City, but he also helped lead a spiritual revival. The Book of the Law was read in the presence of all the people, and they confirmed their covenant with the Lord.

Read Nehemiah 9. List all of the things the people acknowledge about God.

The Prophet Joel:

11. Read Joel 1. [While the date of Joel's prophetic message is questioned, most scholars attribute it to the early post-exilic time.] How do you see Judah, once again, falling into sin and disobedience?

What does Joel call the people to do?

12. ★ **For a Deeper Dive:** Joel often spoke of "the day of the Lord." Read Joel 2:28-32. Why should believers in God's promises not be fearful of that day?

The book of Esther:

[Author's Note: After the exile into Babylon, Persia, who had released the southern kingdom of Judah from captivity, had become the dominant empire. Many of the Jewish exiles remained in Persia rather than returning to Judah and its capital, Jerusalem. The book of Esther takes place during the Persian reign of Ahasuerus. The book of Esther is an exciting account of how one woman was used by God to save the Jewish people from extermination. If time allows during your study this week, read Esther in its entirety.]

13. Read Esther 2. Who were Mordecai and Esther, and why were they no longer in Jerusalem?

How did Esther (a Jew) become queen in Persia, a pagan nation?

14. Read Esther 3:1-6. Who was Haman, and what did he plot?

If Haman's plot was successful, how would it have affected God's covenant with Abraham?

15. Read Esther 4. How did Esther's cousin, Mordecai help save the people? Why could Mordecai say, "For if you keep silent at this time, relief and deliverance will rise for the Jews from another place" (Esther 4:14)?

What does his comment tell us about Mordecai's faith?

Do you believe Esther had faith in God? Why or why not?

16. Despite seemingly insurmountable obstacles and circumstances, Esther was able to save the Jewish people. You will note that God's name is never mentioned in the book of Esther. However, as you read through the historical narrative, where can you see God's sovereign hand?

How might the reminder that God would always preserve His people serve to encourage them as they awaited the coming of the Savior and Messiah?

The Prophet Malachi

17. The Old Testament ends with the book of Malachi. While the Temple was rebuilt and a remnant had returned to Jerusalem, the people continued to disobey, and God's promises had yet to be fulfilled. Malachi pronounced hope that would come in the form of a messenger. Read carefully Malachi 3:1. Who do you think this prophecy references?

18. By this time in HIStory, the Jews had faced the possibility of extinction from many enemies. Recount them. How is it possible that God's people still existed by the time the last prophet, Malachi, spoke?

    What does the preservation of God's people tell you about His commitment to His promise?

SUMMARY WEEK 20

HIStory continues...

EZEKIEL prophesied to the fragments of a shattered nation. While condemning the false shepherds and priests in Jerusalem, he did offer hope by speaking of the true Messiah who would be the true Shepherd of His people. At the end of seventy years, God's people were released from Babylonian captivity. The Lord had told Isaiah that Cyrus would restore His city and free His captive people but not for a ransom. The Persian king, Cyrus, fulfilled the prophecy only one year into his reign over Babylon. Even though Cyrus was not a Jew, God used him to free His people from the Babylonians.

After the Babylonian exile, the people were called to return to the Promised Land. They were to return to Jerusalem and rebuild the Temple, God's dwelling place. They were to restore worship. Incredibly, despite seventy years of captivity, God's people had the financial means to accomplish this due to the order of Cyrus and God's intervention.

Cyrus did more than simply free God's people. He returned all of the items stolen from the Temple when Jerusalem was captured. He also commanded the Babylonians who lived near Jewish survivors: "And let each survivor, in whatever place he sojourns, be assisted by the men of his place with silver and gold, with goods and with beasts, besides freewill offerings for the house of God that is in Jerusalem" (Ezra 1:4). God used nations of the world to fulfill His purposes. He orchestrated the events of history to fulfill His promise to His people. He demonstrated His sovereignty again and again. Every prophecy that God gave about Israel/Judah (His people) that could have happened at this point in history had happened. The Bible records it, and the history books confirm it.

The book of ESTHER is another example of how God would protect His people through His divine providence. When threatened with destruction, God's people were saved through a humble and available servant—Esther.

JOEL warned Judah during a plague of locusts of another future devastation that would come if they didn't repent for their sinfulness. He saw the plague as a precursor or a picture of an even greater judgment by God on the nation. He referred to the time of future judgment as "the day of the Lord." It would be a final reckoning of sinful man with God.

God continued to send His spokesmen to Israel after they were released from exile. EZRA, who was a prophet and priest, led the first group of Jews back to the Promised Land.

NEHEMIAH led the second group back. He also led the people to rebuild the walls around Jerusalem for its protection.

HAGGAI moved the people to action to rebuild the Temple. His message was simple—build the Temple in order to restore the system of sacrifice and atonement. Until the Savior came, the Temple would continue to be God's provision to dwell with His people.

ZECHARIAH looked beyond the present Temple to the Messiah and the spiritual temple of God. He had many prophetic visions of the coming King and foretold that one day the King would ride on a donkey into Jerusalem: "Rejoice greatly, O daughter of Zion! Shout aloud, O daughter of Jerusalem! Behold, your king is coming to you; righteous and having salvation is he, humble and mounted on a donkey, on a colt, the foal of a donkey" (Zechariah 9:9).

And finally, the last prophet MALACHI cried out against the corruption of Israel. Worship and morality were once again in a state of decay. This would be God's last message for a long time. The essence of the message was for God's people to keep the Law of Moses and watch for the coming of Elijah the prophet before the great and terrible day of the Lord. And then silence. God was quiet.

The Bible doesn't record any events that transpired for the four hundred years after the prophet Malachi. History records that God's people faced horrible times, first at the hands of the Greeks and then the Romans. God's people demonstrated time and time again that they couldn't fully obey God's laws, and there were consequences for their disobedience. Does the absence of prophets or God's Word mean that God was absent? Certainly not, but His timing is not ours, and history continued just as God said. Against all odds, the people of Judah were saved. God could keep His promise. Despite the oppression of many nations during the course of their history, this group of people—God's chosen—were preserved.

The Old Testament concluded, but how would the story end? Was there one from the tribe of Judah who would be born and rise as King and Savior? Would there be one who could atone for their sins and serve as a final sacrifice? Would there be one from whom the nations would be blessed? Would the promise to rid the world of Satan be kept?

Personal Application

Consider all the miraculous events in the Old Testament from creation through the return to Jerusalem. What have you learned about God from these stories? How does recalling these events help you "know" that God is the Lord God?

What does it mean to you that God wants you to know Him?

The rebuilding of the Temple had deep significance for the people of Israel. It meant that there was a place that they could come into God's presence and make atonement for their sins through the blood sacrifice of animals. The building of the wall also demonstrated how they were to value and protect God's presence among them. It was meant to be a physical picture of a future spiritual reality. How much do you value God's presence in your life? How do you protect it?

Despite the fact God is not mentioned in the Book of Esther, it is clear that God's hand was instrumental in selecting her "for such a time as this" to save the Jews from extinction. How does seeing God use an "ordinary" individual for such an important mission encourage you to look at your own circumstances to see if perhaps God is calling you for some purpose?

There were 400 years of silence from God after the last of the divine prophets. God's people had to wait. How does waiting on God affect your faith? Have you ever doubted God's love for you during times of waiting, disappointments or suffering?

Additional Notes:

WEEK 21:
Christ is Born

"...I bring you great joy that will be for all the people."

– LUKE 2:10b

Scripture: Read Luke 1–2

1. What was the purpose of Luke's writing? What do you learn about the authenticity of his writing from Luke 1:1–4?

2. ★ **For a Deeper Dive:** If you have access to a study Bible, read about the history of the Jewish people during the time after Malachi until the events described in Luke 1 and 2. How many years have transpired? Describe the historical setting at the time the Promised Savior is born.

    In Galatians 4:4 it is recorded that "when the fullness of time had come, God sent forth his Son, born of woman, born under the law, to redeem those who were under the law, so that we might receive adoption as sons." How might God have been preparing the people for the coming of the promised Savior?

3. The Jewish people had waited a long time for the full fulfillment of the promise to Abraham? See Genesis 22:16–18. How might their faith have been affected?

4. Complete the chart below from Luke 1:

	ZECHARIAH	MARY
What do you learn about them?		
What does this tell you about who God chooses to use for His purposes?		
Visitor		
Promise		
Human obstacle to fulfillment		
Their response		
How would you describe their faith? Explain.		(See also Mary's Song in Luke 1:46-56)

5. Mary and Zechariah responded differently to the angel. What do their responses demonstrate about trusting God?

6. What did Mary know about God as articulated in her song of praise in Luke 1:46-56? What is particularly meaningful to you?

7. Read Matthew 1:18-25. What does this passage reveal about Joseph?

What two names shall be given to the Child? What do these names tell you about Him?

8. Read Luke 1:18-20 along with Zechariah's prophecy in Luke 1:67-79. How has Zechariah's faith changed?

9. What do you learn about John the Baptist's future mission from the prophecy in Luke 1:76-79?

Who is Zechariah referring to in Luke 1:79?

10. Read Luke 1:32-33 as well as Zechariah's prophecy in 1:67-75. What do you learn about the promised Child? What will be His mission?

How might this be related to the Old Testament promise in 2 Samuel 7:12-13, 16?

11. How is God's mercy associated with the promise of salvation?

12. Both Luke and Matthew indicate the place of birth of the Child as Bethlehem. Why is this important? See Micah 5:2.

13. Why is it significant that the promised Savior is born in a lowly manger versus a palace?

14. Read about the birth of Jesus Christ in Luke 2:8-20. To whom was the angelic announcement made? Describe them.

    Why do you think the angel appeared to them?

15. Why was the announcement good news of great joy for all the people?

16. What did the shepherds do after hearing the news? What does their response say about them?

17. What "things" did Mary treasure and ponder in her heart as noted in Luke 2:19? Why?

18. Read Luke 2:22–38. Who was Simeon?

How does his prophecy compare to Zechariah's in Luke 1:77-79?

19. ★ **For a Deeper Dive:** What events do you think Simeon was referring to in Luke 2:34-35?

20. How does Anna's response to Jesus demonstrate her faith?

21. Think of all of the different responses to the arrival of the Savior you studied this week. How are they similar? How do they differ? (Mary, Zechariah, the shepherds, Elizabeth, Simeon, Anna, John the Baptist in utero)

SUMMARY WEEK 21

HIStory continues...

Malachi, the last prophet, spoke of one who would come before the Savior. "Behold, I send my messenger, and he will prepare the way before me" (Malachi 3:1a). Now four hundred years later, John the Baptist was born to Elizabeth. His father, Zechariah, was filled with the Holy Spirit and announced that John the Baptist would "...go before the Lord to prepare his ways, to give knowledge of salvation to his people in the forgiveness of their sins" (Luke 1:76–77). John the Baptist would preach repentance and prepare the hearts of his listeners to receive the coming Savior, just as it was foretold.

Then one day, an angel of God visited a young woman named Mary. The angel told Mary she would bear a son, that he would be called Jesus, and that He would be great and would be called the Son of the Most High. Mary wondered how this could be? She was a virgin and had not yet married Joseph. The angel answered her: "...The Holy Spirit will come upon you, and the power of the Most High will overshadow you..." (Luke 1:35).

The prophet Isaiah made the declaration that the long- awaited Savior had to be born of a virgin. This was one of the first evidentiary requirements. But the Savior had to be born of a virgin for another reason as well. Since the time of the sin of Adam and Eve, offspring were born in the image of man, not of God. The image of God had been scarred by sin. In order for the Messiah to save the world and take on the sin of humankind, He Himself would have to be without sin. He'd have to be unblemished and couldn't have a sin nature. He had to be born of a virgin. Mary—blessed among women—was chosen to give birth to this child. In faith, she proclaimed: "...Behold, I am the servant of the Lord; let it be to me according to your word" (Luke 1:38a).

A decree had gone out from Caesar Augustus requiring all newborns to be registered in the town of their lineage. Joseph, Mary's betrothed, was from the lineage of David, the tribe of Judah, and the city of Bethlehem. As the baby's birth was approaching, Mary and Joseph traveled from their home in Nazareth to Bethlehem to register in accordance with the decree.

And while they were there, the time came for her to give birth. And she gave birth to her firstborn son and wrapped him in swaddling cloths and laid him in a manger, because there was no place for them in the inn. (Luke 2:6–7)

Remarkably, many events transpired and came together so that Jesus was born in the little town of Bethlehem in fulfillment of the Scriptures. A thousand years previously, a promise had been made to David that through his lineage he would reign forever. Hope had been vanishing, patience had waned, but then a child was born. There were shepherds out in the field. An angel appeared to them, and God's glory shone around them.

And the angel said to them, "Fear not, for behold, I bring you good news of great joy that will be for all the people. For unto you is born this day in the city of David a Savior, who is Christ the Lord. And this will be a sign for you: you will find a baby wrapped in swaddling cloths and lying in a manger." And suddenly there was with the angel a multitude of the heavenly host praising God and saying, "Glory to God in the highest, and on earth peace among those with whom he is pleased!" (Luke 2:10–14)

After thousands of years of waiting, but in God's perfect timing, the Savior had been born.

Personal Application

Think of all the various responses to the arrival of the Promised Savior. Which one do you relate to the most? Explain.

Imagine yourself in Mary and Joseph's situation. Do you think you could have responded to the angel, "Behold, I am the servant of the Lord; let it be to me according your your word" (Luke 1:38) as Mary did? Explain.

Do you model this attitude now? In other words, do you graciously accept the unfolding of God's plan for your life? Why or why not?

If your original response to the Savior was written down in a book, what would it say?

How can God use your testimony to draw others to Himself?

Reread the key verse for this week, Luke 2:10, "Fear not, for behold, I bring you good news of great joy that will be for all the people." How is the arrival of the promised Savior good news of great joy for you personally?

The gospel writer, Luke, was a gentile physician. While he was certainly trained in the academic languages, the majority of his account was written in common-man Greek language. How does this insight expand your understanding that salvation had come for all people, not just the Jews?

Reflect on the profoundness of the fact that God was made man, and was born in a manger to be salvation for all. How does this differ from other religions? What does this mean to you?

Additional Notes:

WEEK 22:
Jesus the King

"Where is he who has been born king of the Jews?..."

– **MATTHEW 2:2A**

Scripture: Select passages from Matthew

Complete the chart below:

OLD TESTAMENT PROMISE	FULFILLMENT	
Genesis 12:1-3 2 Samuel 7:12-13	Matthew 1:1-17	The King's familial _____
Isaiah 7:14 Micah 5:2 Numbers 24:17	Matthew 1-2	The King's virgin _____
Hosea 11:1	Matthew 2:19-23	The King's journey from _____
Zechariah 9:9	Matthew 21:1-11	The King's entry into _____
Isaiah 53:5	Matthew 27:26-31	The King's _____

(For an indepth study of the prophecies fulfilled by Jesus, you may want to read through Isaiah 53 and compare it with Matthew 26 and 27)

1. In light of all of the above, how effectively did Matthew present the case that Jesus was the promised King?

2. What question did the Magi ask in Matthew 2:1-12?

Compare the Magi's reaction to Herod's reaction. Why was Herod threatened?

3. In your study of the Old Testament, what did you learn about the kings of both the northern Kingdom of Israel and the southern Kingdom of Judah? Refer back to the Israelites desire for a king in 1 Samuel 8:19-20. How well did the human kings help the Israelites?

4. Matthew was primarily a witness of Christ for the Jews. He wanted to show them that Jesus was the long-awaited, promised King. What phrase is repeated over and over again in his gospel? See Matthew 4:17; 5:3, 10, 20; 7:21; 10:7; 19:23; 22:2; 23:13.

5. Read Matthew 5–7. Jesus preached about the present reality of the Kingdom of heaven which had been ushered in with His coming. What do you learn about the Kingdom of Heaven in these chapters?

How is this Kingdom different from the world?

6. Read carefully the Beatitudes in Matthew 5:2-11. Use a Bible commentary or dictionary for more insight.

BLESSED ARE…	MEANING	PROMISE/HOPE
The poor in spirit	Poor in spirit = to recognize your "spiritual bankruptcy" and inability to save yourself from your sin	Theirs is the kingdom of heaven
Those who mourn		
The meek		
Those who hunger and thirst for righteousness		
The merciful		
The pure in heart		
Peacemakers		
Those who are persecuted for righteousness sake		
You when others revile/ persecute you		

a. Define the word "blessed." Use a bible dictionary or concordance.

b. According to Jesus' description of the kingdom of heaven, how can we rejoice and be glad as suggested in Matthew 5:12?

c. ★ **For a Deeper Dive:** How do you see the Beatitudes build on each other?

7. Jesus spoke in parables to give His followers "secrets of the kingdom of heaven" (Matthew 13:11). Select one or two of the parables below. What do you learn about the present kingdom from the parables?

    a. Matthew 13:18-23

    b. Matthew 13:24-30; 36-43

    c. Matthew 13:31-32

    d. Matthew 13:33

    e. Matthew 13:47-50

8. How is the Kingdom of heaven both a present reality and a future hope?

    ★ **For a Deeper Dive:** See Luke 19:11-12; Daniel 2:44; 7:13-14, 22; Revelation 11:15, 19:11-16; Matthew 26:29.

9. The Jews were looking for a political leader at the time Christ was born. How might they have been disappointed in the Kingship of Christ?

Where else in HIStory have people been disappointed with God as their King? (Hint: See week 13). As a refresher, how did God respond to the Israelites request for an earthly king?

10. Remembering the purpose of the Law, what does it mean that Jesus came to fulfill the Law? See Matthew 5:17-20.

11. Who will be called great in the Kingdom of Heaven?

SUMMARY WEEK 22

HIStory continues...

We know about Jesus' birth, life, ministry, death, and resurrection through the four gospel accounts of Matthew, Mark, Luke, and John. Each speaks to a different audience, and by this, we know the Good News that the Savior had come for all—Jews and Gentiles. While there are four gospel accounts from four different men, there are no inconsistencies. While each gospel adds different details to the story—none conflict. This is important. If the stories were identical, it would be evidence of a conspiracy. It's by their differences we know they're true.

MATTHEW's audience was Jewish. He knew that the focus of his evidence had to be related to the kingship of the Savior for the prophets had spoken of the coming Jewish king. Matthew's Gospel included evidence that Jesus fulfilled the required kingly lineage. The people had kept genealogical records in the Temple so the promised Savior could be linked to the tribe of Judah. Matthew gives the lineage of Jesus back through Abraham.

Not only was the Savior's lineage predicted and that He would be born in Bethlehem, but it was prophesied that "...a star shall come out of Jacob, and a scepter shall rise out of Israel..." (Numbers 24:17). After Jesus was born, "...wise men from the east came to Jerusalem, saying, "...Where is he who has been born king of the Jews? For we saw his star when it rose and have come to worship him" (Matthew 2:1–2). They weren't Jewish, and yet the wise men somehow knew the promises given by the prophets, including the one regarding the celestial announcement. They saw the star and made the connection between the star and the King.

Isaiah foretold there would be homage for the coming King from foreign nations and they would bear gold and incense. And indeed, these wise men from the east who came to worship Jesus as King offered Him gifts of gold, frankincense, and myrrh.

It was also prophesied that the Messiah would be rejected and despised by many (Isaiah 49:7; 53:3, Daniel 9:26). From the time of His birth, there were reactions of hostility. King Herod wanted the baby Jesus killed. Herod was an evil man who was threatened by the coming of this alleged new King. Herod ordered that all the male children in Bethlehem be killed. History records that Herod had already killed his wife and sons, so why not this baby and the other babies in Bethlehem? An angel forewarned Joseph of Herod's plot. Joseph took Jesus and Mary to Egypt to protect them. After Herod died, an angel again appeared to Joseph instructing him to take Jesus and Mary to Israel. They went to live in the city of Nazareth.

At this time in history the Jews, under Roman authority, wanted a political king who would free them from their oppression. The Israelites' history of kings demonstrated that no human king could rescue them. The physical kingdom of Israel continually fell to more powerful nations as they could not obey the Law of God. A different kind of kingdom was needed and a different kind of king. Matthew wanted to force his readers to see Jesus as The King and worship Him as the Magi did. And Matthew's Gospel records the proclamations of Jesus that would define His Kingdom. It wouldn't be a political kingdom. Jesus came first to establish a spiritual kingdom on earth. The Kingdom of Jesus Christ would be one where:

> *Blessed are the poor in spirit, for theirs is the kingdom of heaven.*
> *Blessed are those who mourn, for they shall be Comforted.*
> *Blessed are the meek, for they shall inherit the earth.*
> *Blessed are those who hunger and thirst for righteousness, for they shall be satisfied.*
> *Blessed are the merciful, for they shall receive mercy.*
> *Blessed are the pure in heart, for they shall see God.*
> *Blessed are the peacemakers, for they shall be called sons of God.*
> *Blessed are those who are persecuted for righteousness sake, for theirs is the kingdom of heaven. Blessed are you when others revile you and persecute you and utter all kinds of evil against you falsely on my account. Rejoice and be glad, for your reward is great in heaven, for so they persecuted the prophets who were before you. (Matthew 5:3–12)*

Throughout the gospel accounts, the authors record the many instances where Jesus was rejected and despised, just as foretold by the prophets. They also record the prophecies that Jesus fulfilled in His birth and life. Despite all this evidence, He was not the kind of king the religious leaders wanted, so unlike the Magi, they failed to worship Him.

Personal Application

Consider all you learned this week, how would you describe "kingdom" living to another person?

Based on Jesus' teachings in chapters 5–7, as well as the parables, what challenges do you personally find in living under the authority of Jesus, the King?

What other "kings" does the world tend to submit to? Is it easier to live under the kingship of the world and its moral authority, or that of Jesus?

What "kings" do you tend to submit to?

How would you answer the question, "Where is he who has been born king of the Jews?" Is He on the throne of your life? Why or why not?

The Kingdom of God is a present reality for those who live under the Kingship of Christ. The Beatitudes describe the character attributes of Kingdom dwellers. Which attributes do you see clearly in your life? Which ones challenge you personally?

Additional Notes:

WEEK 23:
Jesus Performs Miracles

"On that day, when evening had come, he said to them, 'Let us go across to the other side...' And leaving the crowd, they took him with them in the boat, just as he was. And other boats were with him. And a great windstorm arose and the waves were breaking into the boat, so that the boat was already filling. But he was in the stern, asleep on the cushion. And they woke him and said to him, 'Teacher, do you not care that we are perishing? And he awoke and rebuked the wind and said to the sea, 'Peace! Be still!' And the wind ceased, and there was a great calm. He said to them, 'Why are you so afraid? Have you still no faith?' And they were filled with great fear and said to one another, 'Who then is this, that even the wind and the sea obey him'"

- M A R K   4 : 3 5 - 4 1

Scripture: Select passages from the Gospels

1. Define the word "miracle." Use a dictionary if necessary.

    What are some terms in Scripture used to describe a miracle? See Mark 2:12; Luke 19:37; John 3:2; 6:2; 14:11; Matthew 7:22; 11:20.

2. Why did God perform miracles in the Old Testament? See Exodus 14:18 or Isaiah 40:20.

3. Examine the miracles of Jesus below and categorize each section of the chart. (If you have limited time this week, just look up a few miracles in each section in order to determine His overall authority over various areas of creation. This chart is meant to give you a resource for Jesus' miracles.)

	MATTHEW	MARK	LUKE	JOHN
JESUS HAS AUTHORITY OVER _____.				
Jesus heals __a blind man__ .	9:32-34			
Jesus heals _____.		7:31-37		
Jesus heals _____.			13:10-17	
Jesus heals _____.				5:1-15
Jesus heals _____.	9:1-8	2:1-12	5:17-26	
Jesus heals _____.	12:9-14	3:1-6	6:6-11	
Jesus heals _____.	8:16-17	1:32-34	4:40-41	
Jesus heals _____.				9:1-41
Jesus heals _____.		8:22-26		
Jesus heals _____.	20:29-34	10:46-52	18:35-43	
JESUS HAS AUTHORITY OVER _____.				
Jesus heals __the 10 lepers__ .			17:11-19	
Jesus heals _____.	8:1-4	1:40-45	5:12-14	
Jesus heals _____.			14:1-6	
Jesus heals _____.	9:20-22	5:25-34	8:43-48	
Jesus heals _____.			22:50-51	
Jesus heals _____.	8:14-15	1:29-31	4:38-39	
Jesus heals _____.	8:5-13		7:1-10	
Jesus heals _____.				4:46-54

	MATTHEW	MARK	LUKE	JOHN
Jesus heals _____.	14:34-36	6:53-56		

JESUS HAS AUTHORITY OVER _____.

	MATTHEW	MARK	LUKE	JOHN
Jesus casts out ___demons___.	12:22-24			
Jesus delivers _____.	15:21-28	7:24-30		
Jesus heals				.

JESUS HAS AUTHORITY OVER _____.

	MATTHEW	MARK	LUKE	JOHN
Jesus _calms the storm_.	8:23-27	4:37-41	8:22-25	
Jesus _____.	14:25	6:48-51		8:19-21
Jesus _____.	14:15-21	6:35-44	9:12-17	
Jesus _____.	15:32-38	8:1-9		
Jesus _____.			5:4-11	

JESUS HAS AUTHORITY OVER _____.

	MATTHEW	MARK	LUKE	JOHN
Jesus _raises the widow's son_.			7:11-17	
Jesus _____.				11:1-45
Jesus _____.	9:18-26	5:21-43	8:40-56	

4. Considering the broad range of Jesus' miracles, what does this tell you about His authority?

For additional insight see Matthew 8:5-13. What does the Centurion note about Jesus' authority?

5. Read a few of the miracles in each of the categories above. Note the different circumstances and means that Jesus used to perform the miracle. Is there any formula that He used?

6. What do the following verses tell us about why Jesus performed miracles?

   a. Matthew 8:16-17

   b. Mark 1:41

   c. Mark 2:1-12

   d. Mark 16:20

   e. John 5:36

   f. John 3:2

   g. John 20:30-31

7. Fill in the chart below with the various responses to Jesus' miracles.

SCRIPTURE	RESPONSE	NOTES/ OBSERVATIONS
John 6:22–27	They wanted more "bread" (or earthly provisions).	Jesus responds later, "I am the bread of life."
John 2:11		
John 2:23–25		
John 4:48, 54		
John 7:11		
John 7:1–9		
John 12:37–43		
Mark 2:12		
Mark 5:1–7		Who is reacting to Jesus in this narrative?
Matt 11:20–24		
Luke 10:12–15		
John 15:22–25		

8. In light of the passages above, did faith lead to miracles? If so, cite examples.

Did miracles lead to faith? If so, cite examples.

Was faith necessary for Jesus to perform miracles? Support your answer from scripture.

9. Why didn't Jesus' miracles always lead to faith in who He is? What is the problem with faith that is based on miracles alone?

10. Read Mark 2:1-12. How would you answer the question, "Which is easier, to say to the paralytic, 'Your sins are forgiven,' or to say 'Rise take up your bed and walk'?"

What was the point of Jesus' question?

SUMMARY WEEK 23

HIStory continues...

MARK recorded the ministry of Jesus to show that He had come as a Servant/Messiah of the people. He highlighted the teachings of Jesus to demonstrate that Jesus came to call all to follow Him as a disciple. LUKE recorded how Jesus was the universal savior who came to save not only the Israelites but also the gentiles of the world. He presented a very orderly account of Jesus' life and teachings for the stated purpose "that you may have certainty concerning the things you have been taught" (Luke 1:4). Each of the gospels records those events of Jesus' life and ministry, specifically the miracles that He performed, which authenticate the claim that He was the promised Messiah and King.

There are approximately thirty-five separate miracles recorded in the different gospels. They showed that Jesus had power and authority over every aspect of the physical realm—the forces of nature, life, and even death. Jesus' first miracle demonstrated His control over nature. He turned water into wine. Thereafter, He fed 5,000 men with five loaves of bread and two fish. He calmed a storm that threatened the lives of His disciples. He caught a multitude of fish after the professional fishermen had failed. With each miracle, the disciples and followers were forced to ask themselves who Jesus was. How could a mere man do these things? "What sort of man is this, that even winds and sea obey him?" (Matthew 8:27).

Jesus also had control over lives as demonstrated when He healed all kinds of sickness. Sometimes He healed by His touch and sometimes by merely His word. For instance, once a Roman centurion sent elders to Jesus in humility and faith to heal his servant: "...Lord, do not trouble yourself, for I am not worthy to have you come under my roof. Therefore I did not presume to come to you. But say the word, and let my servant be healed" (Luke 7:6–7). Jesus, amazed at this gentile's faith to believe in His authority while also acknowledging that he did not deserve anything from Jesus, healed the servant by merely His word.

Jesus showed compassion for the hurting and marginalized in His midst. Jesus healed blindness, deafness, paralysis, fever, shriveled limbs, hemorrhaging, and leprosy. Even death was subject to His authority. Jesus raised a widow's son, the daughter of Jairus, and Lazarus, after he had been in the ground for three days.

Despite the power Jesus displayed, there were many who questioned His authority. The religious leaders didn't want to believe that Jesus was the promised Messiah. They had a privileged position in the Roman world, and they didn't want that changed. They were threatened by the following that Jesus had amassed and, therefore, wanted to end His ministry. If they could find Him guilty of violating the law, they could stop Him. Doing work on the Sabbath was forbidden, so when Jesus healed a blind man on the Sabbath, they thought they'd finally "caught" Him. All they would need was the testimony of someone to state that Jesus had violated the law. Filled with prejudice, malice, and ignorance, they attempted to intimidate the healed man into stating that Jesus committed a sin—violating the Sabbath. The previously blind man's answer was simple, direct, and dismissed their accusation: He answered, "Whether he is a sinner I do not know. One thing I do know, that though I was blind, now I see" (John 9:25). Undeterred by the opposition, Jesus continued with His miracles and His teachings.

By demonstrating His power over the physical realm, Jesus authenticated His authority over the spiritual. If He could heal and raise the dead, He could certainly forgive sins. Jesus presented His reasoning to the religious scribes in an account in Mark. The gospel records that some men came to Jesus with a paralytic to be healed. With great effort to approach Jesus, they removed the roof above Him, made an opening, and lowered the bed of the paralytic. "And when Jesus saw their faith, he said to the paralytic, 'Son, your sins are forgiven'" (Mark 2:5). The scribes accused Jesus of blaspheming God, for who but God could forgive sins. In response, Jesus said to them: "...Why do you question these things in your hearts? Which is easier, to say to the paralytic, 'Your sins are forgiven,' or to say, 'Rise, take up your bed and walk'? But that you may know that the Son of Man has authority on earth to forgive sins—he said to the paralytic—'I say to you, rise, pick up your bed, and go home'" (Mark 2:8–11). If Jesus could forgive sins, wasn't He claiming and authenticating that He was indeed the promised Savior! Matthew, Mark, Luke, and John recorded these events not merely to provide a biography of Jesus, but to encourage us to have faith in Him as the Messiah and King. For the gospel writers, Jesus was the Messiah who came not only to heal and deliver but also to suffer and die for people's sins.

Personal Application

Think of all of the categories of Jesus' authority you witnessed this week and list them below. (i.e. Jesus has authority over _____.) How may remembering God's ultimate authority over these areas encourage you in your current situations?

Have you ever been amazed at something God has done in your life? Would you call it a miracle?

What effect did it have on your faith?

In Mark 9:14-29 you read about a boy with an unclean spirit. When Jesus arrives he tells the boy's father "All things are possible for one who believes" (v23). The father immediately replies "I believe; help my unbelief!" What does this historical account tell you about the coexistence of faith and doubt?

What does the father's response teach you personally?

All throughout HIStory, we see Jesus' miracles proceeded by doubt, fear, and grumbling. What can you do to assuage your unbelief during times of disappointment and struggles?

How have the miracles recorded in Scripture encouraged your faith in Jesus' deity?

★ **For a Deeper Dive:** There is one ultimate miracle of Christ that is the turning point for mankind—the gift of salvation available to all people! (We'll study this more in depth in a few weeks.) But given what you have read this week about miracles, how may that change how you view being "saved" from sin and death?

Additional Notes:

WEEK 24:
Great I Am

"...But who do you say that I am?"

- MARK 8:29

Scripture: Select passages from the gospel of John.

1. What does John state as the reason for his gospel account according to John 1:7 and 20:30-31?

[Author's Note: Most scholars date the gospel of John after the other gospels (known as the synoptics). False teachers, such as those who believed in gnosticism, had begun to arise in the early Church. Gnostics claimed that salvation comes from divine knowledge rather than faith in Jesus Christ, and they questioned the dual nature of Jesus—His simultaneous humanity and divinity.]

How might this explain John's focus and reason for writing

Read John 1

2. Who is the "Word"? What does this insight add to the account of creation given in Genesis 1?

How does John's prologue in 1:1-18 provide evidence of Jesus' deity?

3. Describe all of the things that you learn about the character and ministry of Jesus from John 1:1-18.

4. How does one become a child of God according to John's gospel? How would you respond to someone who says "we are all children of God"?

5. What other descriptions/names are given of Jesus in this gospel account?

    a. John 4:42 _____

    b. John 10:11 _____

    c. John 10:30 _____

    d. John 11:25-27 _____

    e. John 19:19 _____

    f. John 20:28 _____

    g. John 20:31 _____

6. As a refresher, read Exodus 3:13-14. What was the name that God gave Himself?

    What does this name signify?

    [Author's Note: Jesus used the same name for Himself. Anyone hearing this, would have known that Jesus was claiming to be God. Look at the instances cited below. Read carefully the context in which Jesus spoke. These are not only bold claims, but very personal to us.]

Explain the 7 "I AM" statements in the Gospel of John, and the implications for us.

SCRIPTURE	JESUS NAME / I AM STATEMENT	IMPLICATION FOR US
John 6:35–51	I AM… the bread of life	We will not hunger spiritually
John 8:12	I AM…	
John 10:7–10	I AM…	
John 10:11–18	I AM…	
John 11:25–27 (See also 1 John 5:11–12 and 1 Cor 15:53–57)	I AM…	
John 14:1–7	I AM…	
John 15:1–11	I AM…	

7. How would you define the following descriptions of Jesus' identity?

a. The way

b. The truth

c. The life

Read John 3.

8. Describe all you know about Nicodemus. Why does he come to see Jesus?

9. In your own words, what does it mean to be "born again"? Why is rebirth necessary to enter the kingdom of heaven? Consider Genesis 5:3.

What blessing is given for those who are reborn? How is rebirth similar to our physical birth? How is it different?

How does the promise of rebirth further John's argument that Jesus is divine?

10. Consider who Nicodemus was—a ruler of the Jews. Presumably he knew everything about the Jewish "religion." How does Jesus' explanation of how he could see the kingdom of God differ from "religion"?

11. How does believing in Him differ from believing He existed?

⭐ **For a Deeper Dive:** Read John 7:50 and 19:39 for other references to Nicodemus. While we can only speculate, do you think Nicodemus came to believe Jesus was who he said he was? Why or why not?

12. How did John the Baptist regard Jesus? See John 3:22–35. How did he regard himself and his mission in relation to Jesus?

13. Read John 5:18–47. Jesus makes 7 claims of equality with the Father. Identify them below:

SUMMARY WEEK 24

HIStory continues...

In the Gospel of JOHN, he says there are many miracles performed in the presence of the disciples that aren't included in his accounts, but that he does highlight seven as signs of the deity of Jesus Christ: "But these are written so that you may believe that Jesus is the Christ, the Son of God, and that by believing you may have life in his name" (John 20:31).

One of the other evidences John laid out was the reaction to Jesus. Did those around Him know that He was claiming to be God? On one occasion, Jesus declared, "I and the Father are one" (John 10:30). The religious leaders were ready to stone Him right then for committing blasphemy. They knew He was claiming to be God. "...It is not for a good work that we are going to stone you but for blasphemy, because you, being a man, make yourself God" (John 10:33).

Moreover, Jesus claimed to be God by using for Him, the name that God used for Himself—"I AM." If you'll recall, in the Old Testament book of Exodus, Moses encountered a burning bush in the middle of the wilderness while sheep herding for his father-in-law, Jethro. The voice of God spoke to him out of the fire, giving him a mission to free the Israelites from bondage in Egypt. Moses asked for a sign to give the people when they challenged him: Then Moses said to God, "If I come to the people of Israel and say to them, 'The God of your fathers has sent me to you,' and they ask me, 'What is his name?' what shall I say to them?" God said to Moses, "I am who I am." And he said, "Say this to the people of Israel, 'I am has sent me to you'" (Exodus 3:13–14).

The Jewish people knew that God's divine name was "I AM." If anyone used that name, he was either claiming to be God Himself or blaspheming God. In John's Gospel, he records the seven times that Jesus used this very name, I AM. Jesus is claiming to be God in the flesh when He says:

I AM the Bread of Life. (John 6:35)

I AM the Light of the World. (John 8:12)

I AM the Door. (John 10:9)

I AM the Good Shepherd. (John 10:11)

I AM the Resurrection and the Life. (John 11:25)

I AM the Way, the Truth and the Life. (John 14:6)

I AM the Vine. (John 15:5)

Jesus didn't have to say, "I am God" for those around Him to know that was exactly what He was claiming. Anyone who heard these declarations would know Jesus was claiming to be God in the flesh.

Personal Application

Think of all the metaphors and names that Jesus used to describe who He was. List the two or three that are most meaningful to you, and explain why. Are there any that surprised you? Any that were particularly comforting?

How has your view of God changed based on what you read this week?

Based on John's gospel, how would you answer someone who asked, "Who do you say Jesus is?" How would you support your response with Scripture?

How would you respond to someone who says that Jesus was just a great teacher? What practical difference does it make to you that Jesus is more than just a great teacher?

Have you been born again? If so, spend time this week writing down the events surrounding your decision to become born again (i.e. your testimony). Pray about sharing it with someone this week. If you have not made a decision to believe in Jesus as the Son of God, pray about it or share with someone in your study about your hesitations. What are your obstacles? Continue to pray as you continue with HIStory in the weeks ahead!

Additional Notes:

WEEK 25:
Jesus is Crucified

"So they took Jesus, and he went out, bearing his own cross, to the place called the Place of a Skull, which in aramaic is called Golgotha. There they crucified him, and with him two others, one on either side, and Jesus between them...When Jesus had received the sour wine, he said, 'It is finished,' and he bowed His head and gave up His spirit."

– J O H N   1 9 : 1 6 - 1 8 ,   3 0

Scripture: Read all of Matthew 26–27.

1. What notice did Jesus give to the disciples two days before Passover as recorded in Matt 26:2?

2. What did the woman of Bethany do for Jesus at the house of Simon the leper? See Matthew 26:6-13.

    How does Jesus describe what she did?

    What did she seem to understand that the disciples did not?

3. Jesus tells the disciples that one of them will betray him. What do the disciples say in response?

    How is Judas' response different from the others? What does his response tell you?

4. How was Judas' betrayal a fulfillment of prophecy? See Zechariah 11:12-13.

5. What feast were the Jews preparing to celebrate? What did this feast signify in the Old Testament? See Exodus 12:21-28 for insight.

6. Read the account of the Lord's Supper. After taking the cup, why did Jesus declare, "for this is my blood of the covenant, which is poured out for many for the forgiveness of sins." (Matt 26:28). How was the Old Testament Mosaic covenant confirmed? See Exodus 24:8.

   What correlation do you see between the confirmation of the Old Testament covenants, the Passover, John the Baptist's name for Jesus in John 1:29, and Jesus' declaration?

7. Read John 10:17-18 together with Matthew 26: 36-46. Identify all that Jesus knew before His betrayal, arrest and suffering began?

8. What do you learn about prayer from Jesus?

   What reason did Jesus give to the disciples for them to pray? See Matthew 26:41.

What temptation did He expect them to face?

9. Complete the chart below:

"Who did Jesus stand before? Was it a religious or Roman Tribunal? Note the times of the trials."		DECISION	JESUS' RESPONSE
1st Trial	John 18:12-23, Matt 26:57-58		
2nd Trial	Matt 26:59-75		
3rd Trial	Matt 27:1, Luke 22:66-71		
4th Trial	Matt 27:2-14, John 18:28-38		
5th Trial	Luke 23:7-12		
6th Trial	Matt 27:15-26, John 18:39-19:16		

10. Imagine you are a news reporter assigned to the trials of Jesus. How would you describe the events?

11. Would you report that the trials were fair? Why or why not?

12. What did the Jews find Jesus guilty of? Why? See Mark 14:61-64 and John 19:7.

Lookup the definition of this charge. Under Jewish law what was the punishment for this crime? See Leviticus 24:15-16.

13. Why did the Sanhedrin turn Jesus over to Pilate, the Roman governor? See John 18:28-32.

[Author's Note: While history and Scripture confirm that, at times, the Jews did exercise capital punishment by stoning, they stated to Pilate that "it is not lawful for us to put anyone to death." Scholars have uncovered evidence that during this time the Romans had revoked the right of the Sanhedrin to punish by death.]

14. The Sanhedrin presented to the Roman prosecutor (Pilate) the equivalent of a criminal complaint under Roman law—for sedition—which was a capital crime under Roman law. But Pilate rejected the charge. So, what crime did Jesus go to the cross for? See John 19:12-19.

★ **For a Deeper Dive:** Considering who Jesus truly is (Revelation 19:16), how is this ironic?

15. Read the details of the crucifixion in Matthew 27:27-55. How did these events fulfill the Old Testament prophecies about the Promised Savior?

SCRIPTURE	PROPHECY FULFILLED
Psalm 22:1	
Psalm 22:6-8	
Psalm 22:18	
Psalm 69:21	
Psalm 109:25	
Isaiah 50:6	
Isaiah 53:4-9	
Amos 8:9	

16. ★ **For a Deeper Dive:** What happened to the temple curtain? What is the significance of this event? See Hebrews 9:12, 24; 10:19-20.

Think of the direction of the tear. Why is this insight significant given the height of the curtain?

17. What did Jesus declare before lifting up His spirit? See John 19:30.

What did He mean by this?

How do the following verses help explain His declaration?

a. Jeremiah 31:31-34

b. John 1:29

c. 2 Corinthians 5:17

d. Galatians 2:20

e. Hebrews 10:4-10

18. How did Jesus become the Passover lamb?

19. The Passover lamb's blood was shed for the people of Israel. For whom was Jesus' blood shed? See Romans 5:6-10. (For additional insight see 1 Corinthians 5:7 and Isaiah 53:4-6.)

20. Remember the curse to Satan in Genesis 3:15. How was this fulfilled by Jesus' death on the cross? See Hebrews 2:14.

What does this insight tell you about God's commitment to fulfill His word? See Jeremiah 1:12 for additional insight.

SUMMARY WEEK 25

HIStory continues...

The unconditional covenant given to Abraham had been for a people, a land, and a blessing. In the story, it was now time for the beginning of the fulfillment of the last promise to Abraham—that there would be a blessing for the nations of the world. Through the death of the Savior on the cross, the atonement for our sins would be borne by our Hero.

Jesus was arrested at about midnight in the Garden of Gethsemane, and He was tried six times in only twelve hours before both the religious leaders and the Romans. During His trials, there were at least twenty-seven violations of procedural law. In the religious court, Jesus answered, "I am" to the question, "Are you the Christ, the Son of the Blessed?" (Mark 14:61b). He was charged with blasphemy for claiming to be God. The religious leaders, however, had no authority to execute, so they brought Jesus to the Roman officials. In the Roman court, Jesus was charged with sedition. Each trial was a mockery. They had no official charges or witnesses.

The people yelled, "Crucify Him!" After all, He didn't "look" like the promised king. He didn't "sound" like a king since He was silent when accused. Of course, the prophecies had also said that He would be silent: "He was oppressed, and he was afflicted, yet he opened not his mouth; like a lamb that is led to the slaughter, and like a sheep that before its shearers is silent, so he opened not his mouth" (Isaiah 53:7). He was a man without sin, was never found guilty at law, but went to His death as a criminal.

When God substituted the animal for Isaac outside of what would become Jerusalem, Abraham had named the place "God will provide" because He knew God would provide the sacrifice. The sinfulness of the descendants of Abraham would not stand in the way of God's promise to provide a sacrifice so that we don't have to die and be separated from God.

For Jesus to be the sacrifice, however, He would have to shed His blood on Passover. Since the time of Moses, Israel celebrated how God had saved His people. Each year in Jerusalem, they sacrificed a lamb as atonement for their sins. They offered a sacrifice at 3:00 in the afternoon before Shabbat and the Feast of Unleavened Bread. On the exact hour of the last sacrifice on Passover, Jesus died on the cross; God had put meticulous care into His plan of redemption. His Son became the sacrifice.

There was physical evidence that the separation between God and man was now removed. The veil in the Temple that separated man from God was physically torn in two from top to bottom at the moment of His death. No longer would a priest be needed to intercede for us with God. We could approach the Father ourselves. Jesus became our intercessor and our perfect high priest.

The events of Jesus' life and death were fulfillments of the Old Testament prophecies regarding the promised Savior. He was of the promised lineage; His coming was announced by someone—John the Baptist—who called the people to repentance; He fulfilled the promised birth; and He fulfilled in His life what the prophets had said. During the three years of His adult ministry, Jesus demonstrated His authority as the Son of God through signs and miracles, and He continually spoke about His Kingdom. Finally, in His trial and death, many more of the prophetic words were fulfilled. For example, Isaiah spoke of a suffering servant, many of the prophets talked of a sacrifice, and God, Himself, had said that the serpent would bruise His heel. There would be injury to the promised Savior.

Christ was the perfect final sacrifice. He was innocent. The Bible and history have not recorded one sin that Jesus ever committed. He was God's unblemished Lamb, so He could take on the sins of the world so we could be set free from sin. And the nations—those that believe—are blessed. Hanging on the cross at Calvary, Jesus declared, "It is finished." The sacrifice was made. He died for us, once and for all. By not saving Himself, Jesus became the blood offering. What greater love is there?

Personal Application

In the last few weeks of Jesus' life he was treated terribly (and unfairly!) by many people including those close to him—Peter denied him; Judas betrayed him; the religious leaders sought false testimony against him; the crowds wrongly condemn him; the governor's soldiers mocked him. Yet he knew that His mission was to provide salvation to all people. How have you been wronged or treated unfairly? What does Jesus' example reveal to you about enduring wrongful suffering and forgiveness?

Pilate asked Jesus, "What is truth? (John 18:38). How would you answer that question?

Reflect on all that Jesus accomplished through His death on the cross:

The Cross removes separation (Hebrews 10:19-20)

The Cross defeats sin and death (Colossians 2:14)

The Cross crushes enmity and provide peace (Colossians 1:20)

The Cross makes you a new creation (2 Corinthians 5:17)

The Cross fulfills His promises (Isaiah 53:5)

The Cross destroys fear (Isaiah 12:2)

The Cross reminds us of our promised inheritance (Hebrews 9:15-16)

Which ones have particular meaning for you? Why?

How is the acknowledgment and repentance of sin necessary to receive these benefits?

Consider all that Jesus endured for your sins. How does him dying so you can live impact you spiritually?

Practically?

Additional Notes:

WEEK 26:

Jesus is Risen

"For God so loved the world that He gave his only Son, that whoever believes in Him should not perish but have eternal life."

– JOHN 3:16

Scripture: Read John 20–21

As you do this week's study, consider this question: If it could be proven that Jesus rose from the dead, would you believe Jesus' claim that He was the Son of God?

1. After reading the account of the Resurrection in John, recount this historical event in your own words. Note the people, places, and things spoken.

2. Carefully examine the actions of the following individuals. When did they come to believe that Jesus had risen from the dead? Support your answers with the Scripture. What reasons are given for their slowness of heart to believe?

    Mary

    Peter

    John

Thomas

3. Why is belief in the resurrection essential to the Christian faith? See the following Scripture:

   a. 1 Corinthians 15:14, 17

   b. Romans 4:24-25

   c. Romans 6:9

   d. 1 Corinthians 15:19-20

   Examine some of the evidence for the Resurrection given in the Gospels:

4. Evidence—The Empty Tomb

   a. How secure was the tomb? See Matthew 27:62-66.

   b. The empty tomb: John 20:1-9, (For other references see Matthew 28:6, Luke 24:1-3, Mark 16:2-6)

5. Evidence—The Appearances of Jesus

    a. Matthew 28:9

    b. Luke 24:34

    c. Luke 24:15

    d. John 20:14,16, 18

    e. John 20:19-20, 26, 29

    f. John 21:1, 14

    g. 1 Corinthians 15:6-7

h.   Acts 1:1-4

i.   Acts 9:3-6

6.   Evidence—Changed Lives

Peter:

Before the resurrection—John 18:15-27

After the resurrection—Acts 4:10

James (Jesus' brother):

Before the resurrection—John 7:5

After the resurrection—Acts 1:4, 14; Acts 15:13-21

[Author's Note: According to the first-century Jewish historian, Josephus, James was condemned to death by stoning. (Antiquities of the Jews, Book 20, Chapter 9 sec. 1) Consider also: After Jesus' arrest and crucifixion, most of the disciples fled in fear. Yet 10 out of the 11 Disciples (Judas committed suicide) were martyred for their faith. According to traditions, Peter was crucified upside down; Thomas was skewered; John was boiled in oil but survived.]

What would explain the disciples newly-found boldness after the resurrection?

7. Of all people, why should the disciples have expected Jesus to be resurrected? See Matthew 12:40 (For additional insight see Matthew 16:21, 20:19; Matthew 26:32; Luke 24:6-7.)

8. How did the Old Testament Scriptures prophesy the Resurrection of the Promised Messiah?

    a. Job 19:25-27

    b. Psalm 16:8-11

    c. Psalm 22:19-21

9. After reading the account of the Resurrection in the gospel of John, can you think of any other evidence for the historicity of the account?

10. ★ **For a Deeper Dive:** Read the accounts of the Resurrection in the other gospels. (Matt 28; Mark 16; Luke 24). How do you reconcile them with John's gospel?

11. How does the Resurrection distinguish Jesus from all other "religious" leaders?

12. Many people who didn't want to believe came up with contrary reasons Jesus' body was no longer in the tomb. Can you think of any alternatives to Jesus having risen from the dead? How would you argue against these theories?

13. Jesus asked Mary, "Woman, why are you weeping? Whom are you seeking?" (His first words after rising). How does Jesus' appearance more than answer those questions?

SUMMARY WEEK 26
HIStory continues...

The story of the Savior doesn't end with His death on the cross. If it did, we wouldn't have proof of a blessing, nor would we have the assurance of eternal life.

The Gospel of John tells us that on the third day after the crucifixion, the women who had been with Jesus returned to the tomb. There they found the stone—that had once covered the entrance—had rolled away. The body of Jesus was gone. They were perplexed. The stone was massive and couldn't have rolled away on its own. Could men have come, removed the stone, and stolen the body of Jesus? This was highly improbable in light of the historical fact that the Romans would have carefully guarded the tomb. And would the apostles have had the courage to steal His body? The apostles had already shown themselves to be very fearful. Peter had denied Jesus three times, and only John was at the crucifixion. Would these same men have confronted armed Romans to steal a body? Again, this seems very improbable. The word spread quickly that the tomb was empty. To counter the claim of the resurrection, all someone had to do was produce a body. No one could.

Additionally, Jesus' burial cloths were left neatly folded inside the empty tomb. It's hard to imagine that grave robbers would have taken the time to fold the clothes. So where was the body? Two angels appeared to the women with the answer: "...Why do you seek the living among the dead? He is not here, but has risen. Remember how He told you, while he was still in Galilee, that the Son of Man must be delivered into the hands of sinful men and be crucified and on the third day rise" (Luke 24:5–7).

The empty tomb was just one piece of evidence that Jesus had risen from the dead. He appeared in His resurrected body to hundreds of eyewitnesses. More than five hundred eyewitnesses saw the risen Christ at the same time (1 Corinthians 15:6). Could this many people have had the same hallucination at the same time? Of further significance is the fact that some of the recorded witnesses were women. During this time in history, the testimony of women wasn't allowed in court. Ancient writers, if they were making up the story, wouldn't have included women as witnesses.

The evidence of the truth of the resurrection is supported by the radical change in Jesus' followers. Before Jesus died on the cross, no one was willing to defend this Savior. The followers denied him, and many yelled, "Crucify Him, Crucify Him." The apostles hid behind locked doors. Yet after witnessing the resurrection, many were willing to die for Him. What happened? What changed their attitudes?

Only one answer could explain such a radical change—they had witnessed His power over death. They knew He had risen. While it's true that people through history have died for a lie, no one dies for what they know is a lie. Had it been a lie, the apostles and others would have known. Where was the body? Historical accounts record that ten of the original apostles died as martyrs for Jesus, as did the Apostle Paul. Since that time, countless others have died believing that the resurrection is a historical fact.

Had Jesus stayed in the ground, we'd have no proof of the blessing promised to Abraham. God's plan was for man and woman to bear witness to the resurrection to know that it was true. Jesus demonstrated His power over death. Knowledge of this fact can give us the assurance that we, too, can experience eternal life if we believe in Him and in His story. While the Savior's heel was bruised, He was not destroyed. He lives.

Personal Application

Answer the question posed at the beginning of this week's study: If it could be proven that Jesus rose from the dead, would you believe Jesus' claim that He was the Son of God?

After reading the account of the Resurrection, what evidence do you have to believe it is true? If you have obstacles to believing, discuss them with your group leader.

What did you learn about the Resurrection this week that you didn't know before?

What is the correlation between Jesus' Resurrection and ours? What does His Resurrection mean for you personally?

Job 19:25-27 says, "For I know that my Redeemer lives, and at the last he will stand upon the earth. And after my skin has been thus destroyed, yet in my flesh I shall see God, whom I shall see for myself, and my eyes shall behold, and not another. My heart faints within me!"

How does Job's acknowledgement of a living Redeemer encourage your faith? What hope does it offer you for any trying situations you are experiencing right now?

How would you respond to someone who said, "I don't believe in Jesus' literal resurrection, but I believe in following His teachings"?

How should the Resurrection of Jesus change the way you live?

Additional Notes:

WEEK 27:
Spreading the Gospel

"Now those that were scattered went about preaching the word."

- A C T S   8 : 4

Scripture: Select passages from the book of Acts & the Gospels.

1. Read Matthew 28:16-20 and Acts 1:1-11.

   a. Before Jesus ascended into heaven, what commission did He give His disciples?

   b. What specific instructions does Jesus give with regard to making disciples?

   c. What characteristic of Jesus is mentioned in both of these passages? How might this characteristic impact this command?

   d. Who were the disciples sent to minister to? What does this tell you about the expansion of God's people through the New Covenant?

   e. How does He say they would be equipped for this task?

2. What do you learn about the identity and purpose of the Holy Spirit from the following passages:

   a. Psalm 139:7-8

b. John 14:16

c. John 14:26

d. John 15:26

e. Romans 8:26-27

f. 1 Corinthians 2:10-13

g. Ephesians 4:30

3. What were the first actions of the apostles? See Acts 1:14, 21-26.

4. How would you describe the fellowship of the early believers? See Acts 2:42-47. What lessons can be learned from them?

5. Early in their ministry threats arose against the apostles. List the elements of their prayer in Acts 4:23-31. How can their prayer be a model for sharing the gospel?

From Acts 1–12 (Ministry in Jerusalem, Judea, and Samaria)

6. Identify below the key events which demonstrate the growth, as well as the persecution of the early church:

SCRIPTURE	GROWTH IN THE CHURCH	PERSECUTION IN THE CHURCH
Acts 5:12-16	Apostles performed "many signs and wonders" people held them in high esteem "more than ever believers were added"	
Acts 5:17-32, 40		
Acts 6:8		
Acts 7:54-60		
Acts 8:1-3, 4-5		
Acts 9:1-22		
Acts 10:44-48		
Acts 12:1-2		
Acts 12:24		

How does the growth in the early church begin to fulfill Jesus' reference in Acts 1:8 that the gospel would spread "in Jerusalem and in all Judea and Samaria, and to the end of the earth"?

From Acts 13–28 (Gospel spreads to the end of the earth)

[Author's Note: Beginning in Acts 13, Luke, the author of Acts, traces the ministry and missionary journeys of Paul. As you go through the passages below note what you learn about spreading the Gospel from Paul.]

7. **Paul's 1st Missionary Journey:** Cyprus, Antioch, Iconium and Lystra

   a. Acts 13 recounts Paul's testimony in Antioch to the Jews. Read Acts 13:46–52. Who is Paul called to witness to going forward? Why?

   b. Acts 14:1–2

   c. Acts 14:19–23

   d. Acts 15:1–3, 19–21

   What was the dispute, and was it resolved?

8. **Paul's 2nd Missionary Journey:** Philippi, Thessalonica, Beroea, Athens, and Corinth.

What you learn about spreading the Gospel from Paul?

a. Acts 15:36; 16:5

What led Paul to begin this next journey? What was one of the results of his travels?

b. Acts 16: 6-15

How did the Gospel reach Philippi and therefore, Europe?

c. Acts 16: 25-34

d. Paul and Silas were imprisoned and beaten with rods. How did they react? How did they answer the jailer's question, "Sirs, what must I do to be saved?"

    e.   Acts 17:1-5, 16-17

    f.   What was Paul's method of sharing the Gospel?

What were the different responses to the Gospel message Paul shared?

9.   Paul's 3rd Missionary Journey: Galatia, Phrygia, Ephesus, Macedonia, Toas, Eletus, Tyre, and Caesarea.

    a.   Acts 19:8-10

What more do you learn about Paul's strategy for sharing the Gospel from this account?

    b.   Paul's arrest and appeal to go before Caesar: [Author's Note: The final chapters of Acts describe Paul's travel to Jerusalem. There he was subject to crowd hysteria, persecution, false evidence and ultimately arrest. He testified before the governor in Caesarea, and later Agrippa the king. He appealed to Caesar, and because of his Roman citizenship, the request was granted. After a shipwreck on his way to Rome, he arrived. He was placed under house arrest while he awaited trial.]

10. Describe Paul's defense before Agrippa in Acts 26? How would you describe his approach or methodology?

11. The work of the Spirit of God under the Old Covenant was to anoint God's people for service (Numbers 11:17). The role of the Holy Spirit changed with the Resurrection of Jesus. How did you see the Holy Spirit work in the lives of the apostles as they spread the Gospel?

12. Next week you will study the letters that Paul wrote while in prison. Read ahead in Philippians 1:12–18. How did Paul's imprisonment affect the spread of the Gospel?

13. The book of Acts concludes with Paul in house arrest in Rome. We do not learn about his trial before Caesar. How is Acts not a finished story?

14. Acts is often entitled "Acts of the Apostles." Considering the role of the Holy Spirit is that really an apt title? Why or why not?

SUMMARY WEEK 27

HIStory continues...

After the resurrection, Jesus appeared to witnesses for forty days before He ascended into heaven. Before His ascension, however, He gave instructions to His followers: "Go therefore and make disciples of all nations, baptizing them in the name of the Father and of the Son and of the Holy Spirit, teaching them to observe all that I have commanded you. And behold, I am with you always, to the end of the age" (Matthew 28:19–20).

God's plan was that the gospel message would spread through the witness of His followers. In this way, the nations of the world would be blessed. The book of ACTS records the growth of the early church after Jesus' ascension. It would have seemed a daunting task—to spread to the world the message of hope and the forgiveness of sins, but He also promised them power through the Holy Spirit: "But you will receive power when the Holy Spirit has come upon you, and you will be my witnesses in Jerusalem and in all Judea and Samaria, and to the end of the earth" (Acts 1:8).

Through the power of God's Spirit, the apostles spread the message of the forgiveness of sins. God equipped the early apostles with the ability to perform miracles in order to demonstrate their authority as His witnesses. Peter healed a lame man at the Temple. Stephen performed "great wonders and signs among the people." Philip, while proclaiming the news of Christ, performed many signs including healing the paralyzed.

The church grew despite seemingly insurmountable obstacles—persecution, prison, and even death of the apostles. Nothing could thwart the growth of the church. Lives were transformed by God's Spirit, and many were baptized in the name of Christ.

God also used an unlikely individual for His purposes of spreading the gospel. Saul was a Pharisee (a Jew who strictly adhered to the Law of Moses) from the tribe of Benjamin. He studied under a famous rabbi named Gamaliel and had rejected Christ as the promised Messiah. Because of his zealous beliefs, he was part of those who persecuted the early Christians: "But Saul was ravaging the church, and entering house after house, he dragged off men and women and committed them to prison" (Acts 8:3).

One day, Saul was traveling on the road to Damascus to capture Christians and bring them back to Jerusalem to be killed. A light from heaven shone around Saul. Jesus spoke to him: "...Saul, Saul, why are you persecuting me?" (Acts 9:4). Saul acknowledged that the voice was that of the Lord, and his life was changed. Blinded by the light of the Lord, he followed the Lord's instructions to go see a man named Ananias. Ananias laid hands on Saul; Saul received the Holy Spirit and regained his sight. From that day on, Saul boldly proclaimed Jesus as the Son of God, and his name was changed to Paul. He completely surrendered his life to the Messiah and King.

Paul was given the authority to witness to the world. God's eternal Kingdom began to grow one heart at a time as the gospel spread from Jerusalem to Judea and to Samaria. Paul had three separate missionary journeys, which took him through Asia Minor and Greece. Once a man who persecuted others, Paul received persecution. He was beaten and imprisoned, but he persevered to spread the gospel. At the end of the third journey, Paul was arrested in Caesarea. How then did the gospel get to "the end of the earth?"

Paul knew the Word had to get to Rome, which was the center of the world at the time. There wasn't a single population group that Rome didn't conquer or trade with. If the Roman government could be reached with the gospel, it would be possible to reach "the end of the earth." Standing before the Jewish tribunal, Paul gave a strong defense of the gospel, told of his conversion, and concluded with an appeal to Caesar. He knew if this appeal was granted, he'd be sent to Rome. King Agrippa handed Paul over to a Roman centurion and Paul was discharged to Rome for trial. During the voyage, they encountered a storm and shipwreck, and at times, it seemed that Paul wouldn't get to his destination. But he was promised by an angel of God that he'd be tried in Rome: "... Do not be afraid, Paul; you must stand before Caesar..." (Acts 27:24).

God fulfilled His promise to Paul, and the narrative of the early church appropriately ends with Paul in Rome. As a faithful follower of Christ, Paul "...welcomed all who came to him, proclaiming the kingdom of God and teaching about the Lord Jesus Christ with all boldness and without hindrance" (Acts 28:30–31). The gospel began to spread to the end of the earth.

Personal Application

"And Jesus came and said to them, "All authority in heaven and on earth has been given to me. Go therefore and make disciples of all nations, baptizing them in the name of the Father and of the Son and of the Holy Spirit, teaching them to observe all that I have commanded you. And behold, I am with you always, to the end of the age."

- MATT 28:18-20

The passage above is referred to as The Great Commission, and the primary command in the original Greek language is to "make disciples." In your own words, what does it mean to make disciples?

How has God called you specifically to make disciples in your circle of influence? What steps of faith might you need to take to live out this command more faithfully? Is there an immediate step you can take? Explain below.

(Note: If you aren't sure how God has called you to carry out this command, commit to praying for Him to reveal it to you. Perhaps ask some trusted friends to pray as well.)

Acts 1:8 says "you will receive power when the Holy Spirit has come upon you, and you will be my witnesses." Have you ever experienced the power of the Holy Spirit as you shared the Gospel with someone? If so, write it down below or share with your group.

Think about the other various roles of the Holy Spirit that you studied this week. Are any of particular comfort or reassurance to you? Explain.

What does the story of Saul/Paul teach us about the possibility of the Gospel reaching those with the hardest of hearts?

Is there anyone that you consider "beyond the Gospel" like Paul appeared to be?

How should his conversion story change your attitude about to whom you share the Gospel of Christ?

What can you learn from Paul's example in Acts 28:30-31 about participating in HIStory?

Would you be willing this week to pray for the opportunity to share the Gospel with someone? If so, take a few minutes to do so now, and write a short prayer below.

Before Jesus ascended into heaven, He assured the apostles, "And behold, I am with you always, to the end of the age." (Matthew 28:20). Notice that He did not say, "I will be with you" but rather the presence tense "I am" with you. How does this truth encourage you as you focus on sharing the Gospel?

Additional Notes:

WEEK 28:
Letters of Paul

"Or do you not know that your body is a temple of the Holy Spirit within you, whom you have from God..."

– 1 CORINTHIANS 6:19

Scripture: Select passages from Paul's letters

[Author's Note: The following chart reflects research on the dates and events of Paul's conversion, missionary journeys and imprisonments, and how these events correlate with his letters (or epistles) written to people in the early churches. While the dates may differ slightly in various resources the general sequence is the same.]

Paul's Life Events & Letters

APPROXIMATE YEAR	EVENTS	CHAPTER IN ACTS	PAUL'S LETTERS
34 A.D.	Paul's conversion	9	
37 A.D.	Jerusalem, Tarsus, Syria, Cilicia		
46-47 A.D.	Antioch, Jerusalem	11	
48-49 A.D.	1st Missionary Journey	13–14	Galatians
49-50 A. D.	Jerusalem Council	15	
51-53 A.D.	2nd Missionary Journey (including 18 months in Corinth)	16–18	1 Thessalonians
			2 Thessalonians
53-55 A.D.	3rd Missionary Journey	19–21	1 Corinthians (written in Ephesus)
55-56 A.D.			2 Corinthians
			Romans
57 A.D.	Jerusalem Arrest	22–23	
57-59 A.D.	Prisoner in Caesarea	24–26	
59-60 A.D.	Journey to Rome	27–28	

APPROXIMATE YEAR	EVENTS	CHAPTER IN ACTS	PAUL'S LETTERS
60- ? A.D.	House arrest in Rome	28	Ephesians
			Colossians
			Philemon
			Philippians
			1 Timothy
			Titus
			2 Timothy

Paul's letters present doctrinal truth to the early followers of Christ. This truth is still applicable today. The following Scriptures will give you an overview of the questions that Paul addressed.

1. How does Paul start all of his letters? Do you see any repeating phrases or words?

    What is the significance of this salutation in Paul's letters?

2. Galatians

    a. Why does Paul write to the church in Galatia? See Galatians 1:6-9 and 2:16.

    b. What is the spiritual condition of the church in Galatia? See Galatians 3:1; 4:9; 5:4.

c.   In light of the problem in Galatia, why might Paul have begun his letter with his testimony? See Galatians 1:11-24.

d.   How does Paul answer those in Galatia who claimed that only Jews could be saved? See Galatians 3:7-9.

e.   How are followers of Christ free from the bondage of the Old Testament Law? Galatians 3:10-14; 5:1,13-15.

f.   What did the Old Testament prophet, Ezekiel, promise? See Ezekiel 36:26. How is this promise fulfilled in the lives of believers? See Galatians 5:22-24.

3.   1st and 2nd Thessalonians

a.   What is the condition of the church in Thessalonica? See Thessalonians 1:3-4.

b.   The Old Testament prophets spoke of "the day of the Lord." What more do you learn from Paul about that day in 1 Thessalonians 5:1-11 and 2 Thessalonians 2:3-9.

    c.   How are followers of Christ encouraged to live until the day that Jesus comes again? See 2 Thessalonians 2:13-15.

4.   1st Corinthians

    a.   What is the condition of the church in Corinth? What problem are they are struggling with at the time? See 1 Corinthians 1:10-11; 5:1; 6:5-6.

How can this problem affect the spread of the Gospel and the church's witness for Christ?

    b.   One of the recurrent themes in the Old Testament was that God wanted to dwell among His people. It was for that reason that He commanded them to build the tabernacle and the Temple. How does God dwell with believers under the New Covenant? See 1 Corinthians 6:19-20.

    c.   Paul reminds the Corinthians that Christ's resurrection is an essential aspect of the Gospel. What hope does does that provide followers of Christ? See 1 Corinthians 15:12, 35-49.

5.   2nd Corinthians

    a.   When God created man, He made him in the likeness of Himself. After the fall of Adam and Eve, man and woman no longer reflected the true image of God (Genesis 5:1-3). How is the image of God being restored in the lives of followers of Christ? See 2 Corinthians 3:18.

6. Romans

    Look up the following verses and note what they say about the Gospel.

    a. Romans 3:23

    b. Romans 6:23

    c. Romans 5:8

    d. Romans 10:9

    e. Romans 10:13

    f. Based on your notes above, how would you answer the question "what is the gospel?"

7. Ephesians

    a. Define grace in your own words.

b. How would you explain to someone why it is by grace through faith that we are saved? See Ephesians 2:8-10 for insight.

c. What is the role of "works" in the life of a believer?

d. What is the mystery of Christ? See Ephesians 3:4-6.

Given what you have learned in HIStory about the nation of Israel, why is this important?

8. Colossians

a. What does Paul remind the church in Colossae that the Cross accomplished? See Colossians 1:20.

Why is this significant given what you know about the Tabernacle, the Temple, and the atonement of sins?

b. What does it mean to "walk in a manner worthy of the Lord"? See Colossians 1:9-14.

   c. How does Paul describe a believer's new life in Christ? See Colossians 3:12-17.

9. Philemon

The short letter of Philemon is an appeal by Paul to Philemon (a church host) to receive back a runaway slave named Onesimus. While Paul was obliged to act within the confines of the law of the time, he urged Philemon to recognize Onesimus as a brother in Christ.

   a. How should the new covenant of grace affect our relationships with one another?

10. Philippians

The life of a follower of Christ is not void of suffering. How does Paul exhort believers to live amidst their trials in the verses below?

   a. Philippians 2:17-18

   b. Philippians 3:1

   c. Philippians 3:14

   d. Philippians 4:4

11. 1st and 2nd Timothy, & Titus

Paul wrote these letters to Timothy and Titus who were leaders in their respective churches. For this reason they are known as the Pastoral Epistles.

a. Paul continually warned those in the church against "false teachers." Use the chart below to note how Paul describes false teachers.

SCRIPTURE	DESCRIPTION OF FALSE TEACHERS
1 Tim 1:3-4	"different doctrine" "devote themselves to myths and endless genealogies" "promote speculations rather than the stewardship from God that is by faith"
1 Tim 6:3-5	
1 Tim 6:20	
2 Tim 1:13-14	
2 Tim 4:1-4	
Titus 2:1	

b. Why are false teachers so dangerous?

c. How does Paul encourage the church to "hold firm" to sound doctrine?

    i. 1 Timothy 4:13-16

    ii. 2 Timothy 3:14-17

    iii. Titus 2:1-8

SUMMARY WEEK 28

HIStory continues...

Throughout Paul's journeys, as well as during times of imprisonment, he maintained contact with the churches he established. Paul's letters include I and II THESSALONIANS, I and II CORINTHIANS, EPHESIANS, PHILIPPIANS, COLOSSIANS, GALATIANS, ROMANS, PHILEMON, I and II TIMOTHY and TITUS. His letters proclaimed the gospel, encouraged the early Christians, but also corrected false teaching.

Because many of the early believers were Jewish, they wanted to keep the Old Testament dietary laws, as well as circumcision, as proof of their faith so they might be saved. Paul's teachings established that it was by faith alone that we are saved. The law's purpose was to point to our sinfulness. If we need to keep the law perfectly to come into God's presence, we would all fall short: "For by grace you have been saved through faith. And this is not your own doing; it is the gift of God, not a result of works, so that no one may boast" (Ephesians 2:8–9).

The question arose, however, could people freely sin because they were forgiven? Paul explained that they'd been set free from sin. For those who believe that Jesus Christ is the Son of God and our Savior, His Spirit comes and dwells within them. The hearts of believers become permanent "spiritual" temples for His presence. This was in fulfillment of God's promise through the prophet, Ezekiel: "And I will give you a new heart, and a new spirit I will put within you..." (Ezekiel 36:26).

This new heart and Spirit of God would direct believers to live righteously. As believers listen and obey the promptings of that Spirit, there would be a natural outpouring of God's attributes. "But the fruit of the Spirit is love, joy, peace, patience, kindness, goodness, faithfulness, gentleness, self-control; against such things there is no law. And those who belong to Christ Jesus have crucified the flesh with its passions and desires" (Galatians 5:22–24).

We see in the books of the New Testament that the Spirit of God transformed lives, giving them boldness and the ability to persevere. These writings, inspired by God, continue to be God's Word to us. Paul's letters demonstrate how we're called to live according to God's original intention—reflecting His image, worshiping Him alone, and making Him ruler over our lives.

Personal Application

Consider some of the contents and themes of Paul's letters:

He reminded them of the Gospel

He admonished, or reprimanded, their ungodly behaviors (sexual immorality, quarreling in the church, etc.)

He taught them on relevant issues (marriage, the law vs. grace, the Lord's supper, the body of Christ, false teachers, etc.)

He encouraged them and exhorted them in their faith

While each of the letters were addressed to a specific audience with a specific message, Paul's overarching approach to guiding them can serve as a model for a healthy, biblical community. Now consider your biblical community. How does it compare? Explain.

Meditate on the reality that your body is the temple of God's Spirit. What does it mean that God wants to abide in you and have constant fellowship with you?

What practical effects should this have on the way you live? Consider that the temple in the Old Testament reflected the glory of God. How can you reflect God's glory to an unbelieving world?

Is there an area of your life that you are struggling to reflect God's image? Pray about it this week.

"Now you are the body of Christ and individually members of it." 1 Corinthians 12:27

How should this statement inspire unity in the church? Do you believe that you are a valuable member of the body of Christ? What gifts do you have that God wants you to use for His purposes?

Consider HIStory throughout the Old Testament, and the constant struggle of God's people to be obedient. Now think of the New Covenant and being "saved by grace through faith." How do grace, faith, and obedience to God work together in your life? Do you rely on one more than the others?

Additional Notes:

WEEK 29:
Body of Believers

"First of all, then, I urge that supplications, prayers, intercessions, and thanksgivings be made for all people, for kings and all who are in high positions, that we may lead a peaceful and quiet life, godly and dignified in every way. This is good and it is pleasing in the sight of God our Savior, who desires all people to be saved and to come to the knowledge of the truth."

- 1 T I M O T H Y   2 : 1 - 4

Scripture: Select passages from letters of the apostles (James, 1 and 2 Peter, 1, 2 & 3 John, Jude, and Hebrews)

[Author's Note: There are many doctrinal truths in the general epistles. This week's lesson will focus on how the body of believers are called to persevere in the faith and to advance the Kingdom of God. As you go through the study, consider how you can be used to "write" HIStory with your life, and the role faith plays in that call.]

1. James [Author's Note: James was the half-brother of Jesus (Matthew 13:55). His letter was probably the earliest of the New Testament writings.]

   a. How is a follower of Christ to act during trials? What might be the purpose of trials? What is the reward? James 1:2-15

   What does it say we should ask for specifically? Why would that be important during seasons of trials?

   b. How are works related to faith? See James 2:14-26. List the two examples from the Old Testament mentioned and how their faith and actions worked together.

   c. Read James 5:13-18. What do you learn about prayer?

What different prayers are mentioned in these verses? How is prayer essential in the life of a follower of Christ?

2. 1st Peter

   a. Read 1 Peter 2:10–3:7. What did Peter mean that believers are "exiles"? As exiles, how can we glorify God?

   b. How might these admonitions of submission advance God's kingdom?

   c. Have you ever experienced suffering as a Christian? What encouragement can you find in these verses? 1 Peter 4:12-19

3. 2nd Peter

   a. Read 2 Peter 1:3-15. What does Peter encourage followers of Christ to "make every effort" to do in verse 4?

   What do these qualities prevent?

What does verse 10 say to "be all the more diligent" to do?

b. Read 2 Peter 2:1-3. What are the schemes of the false prophets?

c. The letters contain many warnings about false prophets. Based on what you read last week and in 2 Peter, why would this have been such an important issue in the early church, as the Gospel was spreading?

4. 1st John

a. Read 1 John 5:13. Why does John write this letter?

b. How can we be assured that we are followers of Christ? See the following verses for more insight.

i. 1 John 2:3-6

ii. 1 John 2:9-11

iii. 1 John 2:15-17

  iv. 1 John 3:11-15

  c. What role does obedience to God's Word play in the walk of faith?

5. Read 2nd John (It's only 1 chapter!)

  a. Define "love" according to John.

6. Read 3rd John

  a. What does John say brings him "no greater joy"?

  b. What does it mean to "walk in the truth"?

7. Read Jude 1

  a. Why does Jude feel compelled to write this letter?

  b. What does he warn the recipients about in verse 4?

What have you learned from HIStory about "the way of Cain"? (See week three, question 16).

c. How can you protect yourself and others from "way of Cain"? Note the instructions in verses 20-21.

8. Hebrews

[Author's Note: While the author of Hebrews is the subject of scholarly debate, the audience is certain. He spoke to Jewish believers who knew the Old Testament prophets and God's promises. The book of Hebrews is meant to remind them how Jesus Christ is the fulfillment of all that was promised. With this assurance, they are exhorted to hold on to their faith and encourage one another.]

a. How is Christ's supremacy (or superiority to all) revealed?

How would you answer the question, "Who is Christ?" See Hebrews 1:1-4; 2:14-18; 3:5-6; 4:14-16.

b. List all the ways Jesus is a the ultimate "high priest." See Hebrews 7:23-27; 9:11-14.

c. Read Hebrews 10 in its entirety. How is Jesus' sacrifice superior to the sacrifices of bulls and goats?

d.   In response to what Jesus has done for you, what commands are given? See Hebrews 10:22-25.

e.   Read Hebrews 13:1-8. List the exhortations given.

SUMMARY WEEK 29

HIStory continues...

Practical instructions to the early church include the letters of JAMES, I and II PETER, I, II, and III JOHN, and JUDE. They also wrote letters to the followers of the Savior instructing each to persevere in the faith, to live as Christ lived, as a servant—loving and caring for others. They supported Jesus' own instructions: "A new commandment I give to you, that you love one another: just as I have loved you, you also are to love one another" (John 13:34). We, too, are called to "love one another" today.

All of the New Testament is meant to instruct us. It continues to be God's Word to every follower of Christ: "But be doers of the word, and not hearers only, deceiving yourselves" (James 1:22). What is written in the Bible is only part of God's story. We have the opportunity to write the continuation of God's story of blessing and salvation for the world. God has included us in His story, and we have a part to play. This means that as His followers, we can continue to spread the message of the gospel as we testify to the world.

One of the last letters in the New Testament was to the HEBREWS. The author wanted to remind us that we should put our faith in Christ alone. He is the greatest rescuer, for He is the Son of God; He is the greatest High Priest, for although tempted, He is without sin and can sympathize with our weaknesses; He brings a better covenant, for it is by His grace that we receive its benefits; and He is the perfect sacrifice for the atonement for sins, for His death on the cross was once and for all. As we write His story with our lives, we are exhorted to be intentional about our faith.

First, we are told: "Let us draw near with a true heart in full assurance of faith, with our hearts sprinkled clean from an evil conscience and our bodies washed with pure water." This is not a one-time event. Every day, we have the opportunity to come into the presence of God. Then, we are told: "Let us hold fast the confession of our hope without wavering, for he who promised is faithful" (Hebrews 10:23). By remembering that God has delivered on every one of His promises, we can finally: "And let us consider how to stir up one another to love and good works, not neglecting to meet together, as is the habit of some, but encouraging one another, and all the more as you see the Day drawing near" (Hebrews 10:24–25).

While each individual must make his or her own decision to believe that Christ was the promised Savior, as followers, we are part of a body of believers. We become part of God's family: "But to all who did receive him, who believed in his name, he gave the right to become children of God, who were born, not of blood nor of the will of the flesh nor of the will of man, but of God" (John 1:12–13).

When Adam and Eve sinned, their pride had prevented them from putting their faith in God. Rather, they believed the serpent's lie and essentially put their faith in themselves. When we put our faith in Christ, we become His witnesses, joining others throughout the ages to advance His Kingdom here on earth.

Personal Application

"But be doers of the word, and not hearers only, deceiving yourselves. For if anyone is a hearer of the word and not a doer, he is like a man who looks intently at his natural face in a mirror. For he looks at himself and goes away and at once forgets what he was like. But the one who looks into the perfect law, the law of liberty, and perseveres, being no hearer who forgets but a doer who acts, he will be blessed in his doing."

– JAMES 1:22–25

What are practical ways you can be a "doer" of the word? List a few and put a star next to one or two things you want to implement this week.

What is the reward for being a doer of the Word?

Both the Pauline and General epistles contain warning against false teachers. Who are some of the teachers you follow?

What can you personally do to protect yourself from false teaching? What safeguards can you put in place?

Scripture exhorts us to speak the truth in love (Ephesians 4:15). After reading through the epistles, how would you explain that concept to someone?

Between the letters 2 Peter and 1st John, the word knowledge is used almost 30 times. 2 Peter 3:18 says, "But grow in the grace and knowledge of our Lord and Savior Jesus Christ. To Him be glory both now and forever! Amen." How have you grown in grace and knowledge of your Savior through studying HIStory? How do you know God more intimately than you did before? Explain.

How can you continue to regularly grow in your knowledge of the Lord and "supplement your faith" (2 Peter 3:5-8)? What practical disciplines do you need to implement? Explain.

Hebrews ends with a benediction (Hebrews 13:20-21). How can you implement this prayer in your own life?

Think about a product or service that you love. (i.e. your favorite restaurant in town, a must-read book, etc.) Based on how much you "believe" in that particular thing, how comfortable (or bold) do you feel to share it with others?

Now think about your belief in Jesus as your Lord and Savior. How can your belief in HIS power encourage you to share HIStory with others? How are you more equipped to share about this than anything else?

How have you continued to "write" God's HIStory with your own life?

Additional Notes:

WEEK 30:
Book of Revelation

"Behold I am coming soon, bringing my recompense with me, to repay each one for what he has done. I am the Alpha and the Omega, the first and the last, the beginning and the end."

– REVELATION 22:12-13

Scripture: Select passages from Revelation

[Author's Note: John received this Revelation while in exile on the island of Patmos. He had lived a long life preaching the Gospel, but was persecuted for his faith. Revelation may seem difficult to understand as it is filled with visions and symbolism. And yet, it is filled with promises for an eternal future. You are encouraged to avoid getting caught in the details, but rather focus on the glorious hope that it was meant to provide.]

Read Revelation 1.

1. Using a dictionary define the word "revelation."

2. What is the purpose of the revelation given to John as indicated in verse 1?

3. ★ **For a Deeper Dive:** While we have seen in our study that there is only one God (Isaiah 44:8; Deuteronomy 6:4; Malachi 6:10; Mark 12:29), there is a triune nature of God. How do you see the three persons of God in Revelation 1?

4. How does verse 1:7 confirm what was promised when Jesus ascended in Acts 1:11? How is this encouraging?

5. What instruction was John given in Revelation 1:11, 19?

6. List everything you learn about Jesus from Revelation 1. What images of Jesus stand out to you?

7. Revelation 2 and 3 include letters to seven churches. At the time John received this revelation, the churches faced intense persecution. The letters were meant to give instructions on how to persevere in the midst of these trials until Jesus comes again. Identify below the problem in the church, the accompanying warning and the promise given. Put a star next to any of the problems still relevant to churches today.

SCRIPTURE	CHURCH	PROBLEM	WARNING	PROMISE
Rev 2:2-7	Ephesus	Abandoned the love you had at first. (v4)	Repent, or I will remove your lampstand. (v5)	To the one who conquers I will grant to eat of the tree of life, which is in the paradise of God. (v7)
Rev 2:8-11				
Rev 2:12-17				
Rev 2:18-28				
Rev 3:1-6				
Rev 3:7-13			Note: This church was the only church that was not given a warning.	
Rev 3:14-22				

[Author's Note: There are several interpretations of Revelation. The theological term, eschatology, is the study of the end times and Jesus' return. The approaches differ as to the timing and literalness of the visions described. For example, the approaches differ as to the literalness and timing of the events in 1 Thessalonians 4:13-18 (termed by some as the rapture), when Jesus will return in relation to the 1000 year reign (known as the millennium), and whether the promise of land to Israel is yet to be fulfilled in a literal manner. For those of you interested, you can take a lifetime to explore and debate. This week, as you conclude HIStory, rather than coming up with a chronology of the events, simply ask yourself—what does God want me to know, and if Jesus were to return today would I be ready?]

8. Complete the "Insights" column in the chart below:

EVENTS	SCRIPTURE	INSIGHTS
Trials and tribulation before Jesus returns	2 Timothy 3:1-9, 13 2 Peter 3:3-4 Matthew 24:23-24; (For additional references you may look at the Old Testament prophecy of Daniel 12 and 2 Thessalonians 2:3-10)	Who will come in the last days? Identify some of the specific events. Do you see any evidence of these events in today's world?
Hope for believers in Christ	Luke 23:39-43 1 Thessalonians 4:13-18 1 Corinthians 15:51-54	How might these verses help give encouragement to you?
Jesus' return	Matthew 24:36 Hebrews 9:28; Acts 1:10-11 Revelation 19:11-21	How do these passages assure you that Jesus is coming again? When is Jesus returning? Describe as best you can what will happen.

EVENTS	SCRIPTURE	INSIGHTS
Destruction of Satan	Revelation 19:19-20 Revelation 20:13-15	How do these passages display God's justice?
Judgment for believers in Christ	Romans 8:1 John 5:24 Romans 14:10; 1 Corinthians 3:9-15 2 Corinthians 5:10 Revelation 11:18	What promise is assured for believers? For what will believers be judged?
Judgment for non-believers	Revelation 6:15-17 Revelation 20:11-15	How will non-believers be judged?
Crowns promised for believers.	1 Corinthians 9:24-25 1 Thessalonians 2:19 2 Timothy 4:8 1 Peter 5:4 Revelation 2:10	Name the crown and to whom it will be given.

9. Believers in Christ are assured of heaven. It is real! What do the following verses tell us about who will be in heaven:

SCRIPTURE	WHO WILL BE IN HEAVEN
Acts 7:49 (for additional references look at Deuteronomy 26:15, Psalm 2:4, Matthew 6:9)	
John 3:16	
Romans 6:23	
Revelation 7:9–12	
Matthew 18:10	

10. How have your heard heaven described by people in the world? How does Revelation 21:1–22:5 paint a different picture of the eternal dwelling place for believers in Christ?

11. What things are absent from heaven?

    a. Revelation 7:16–17

    b. Revelation 21:4

    c. Job 3:17

d.   2 Thessalonians 1:7

e.   Luke 20:36

12.   Read 1 Corinthians 15:35-58. How would you describe our "glorified" bodies? What additional information do we learn from the description of Jesus' resurrected body? See Luke 24:39-43.

13.   ★ **For a Deeper Dive:** Unlike other "histories" HIStory does not end. How is this reality seen in the following verses:

a.   Psalm 23:6

b.   John 10:28

SUMMARY WEEK 30
HIStory continues...

Jesus came to reconcile us to God and to invite us to enter into eternal life. People ask—if Jesus came, why do we still have war, famine, disease, and evil? At times, it feels as though Satan is winning. There is more to the story, however, that's been written but not yet realized. Jesus wants all to choose life, so He waits to come again. Jesus will return and usher in His eternal and peaceful Kingdom. Jesus' death and resurrection assured us of eternal life, but the ultimate destruction of Satan and all evil will take place in the future.

The story of what will happen is written in the book of REVELATION. While in exile on the island of Patmos, the Apostle John was given the Revelation of Jesus Christ by His angel. John bore witness to the Word of God and was instructed to write down the things that would take place in the future.

John received the Revelation in a series of visions. The events he recorded are signs and symbols of what will transpire rather than a chronology of specific events. No one knows with certainty how and when the events will take place, but these things are assured:

Christ will come again.

He will reign forever and ever.

All will know that Jesus is King.

Every knee will bow and every tongue will confess that He is Lord!

Those who die believing in Jesus Christ as the Savior have their names written in The Book of Life.

One day, they will reign with Christ.

"No longer will there be anything accursed, but the throne of God and of the Lamb will be in it, and his servants will worship him. They will see his face, and his name will be on their foreheads. And night will be no more. They will need no light of lamp or sun, for the Lord God will be their light, and they will reign forever and ever." (Revelation 22:3–5)

As believers, our souls immediately enter the presence of God in heaven when we die our physical death on this earth. When Jesus returns the second time, we'll be given a new spiritual body suited to live in a perfect world. God's enemies—including Satan who is the source of evil—will be conquered and thrown in the lake of fire for eternity. The old earth will pass away, and a new heaven and earth will one day be established.

SUMMARY

"Then I saw a new heaven and a new earth, for the first heaven and the first earth had passed away, and the sea was no more. And I saw the holy city, New Jerusalem, coming down out of heaven from God, prepared as a bride adorned for her husband. And I heard a loud voice from the throne saying, "Behold, the dwelling place of God is with man. He will dwell with them, and they will be his people, and God himself will be with them as their God. He will wipe away every tear from their eyes, and death shall be no more, neither shall there be mourning, nor crying, nor pain anymore, for the former things have passed away." (Revelation 21:1–4)

Just as the doors of Noah's ark closed, there will come a time when it's too late to receive God's grace. No one knows the day or the hour when this will occur. But God is patient and He wants all to come to Him. All have a choice to spend eternity in a glorious place called heaven.

Personal Application

At times we can be overwhelmed by the bad things happening in the world, or by our own pain and suffering. How does the message of Revelation provide us with hope?

What descriptions of heaven give you the most joy?

Read 1 Corinthians 13:12; Matthew 5:8; 24:44. Do you know if you are ready to come face to face with God? Explain why or why not.

Philippians 3:20 tells us that our "citizenship is in heaven." While the full realization of the Heavenly Kingdom is yet to come, identify the following kingdom benefits which we can enjoy today, and what they mean to you.

SCRIPTURE	BENEFIT AND ITS BLESSING TO YOU
1 John 3:24	
2 Corinthians 6:16	
2 Corinthians 13:14	
1 Peter 3:12	
John 9:31; 16:23	
Romans 8:26–27, 34	
Hebrews 7:25	
1 John 1:7, 9	
2 Thessalonians 3:3	
Ephesians 1:9	
Ephesians 2:10	

Concluding Application Questions:

How would you describe to someone the "plot" of HIStory from Genesis to Revelation?

How have you seen the Hero, the Savior, throughout HIStory?

How does viewing the Bible as one continuous story affirm your faith?

Jot down your biggest personal applications from HIStory. What has reading His Word taught you about God?

What has the Lord taught you about your heart, your tendencies, or your faith?

The Bible has been described as the Living Word of God. Its contents are unchangeable and inerrant, and it continues to give us guidance and direction no matter what our circumstances. It is God's Word to us, and He wants to speak to you! It is a journey that He has invited you to take. Are you willing to make reading and studying Scripture part of your daily life?

Concluding Reflections

The Bible, read from beginning to end, tells one complete unified story. In Genesis, God created man in His image, but due to man's sinfulness, that image was broken and a gap was created between the Holy and perfect God and man. In order to reconcile God and man, God had the entire story written from the beginning. There is one main plot—God's plan to redeem is the consistent theme of the Bible. And like any good story, the plot has a Hero, or in this case, a Savior.

Throughout the Old Testament, there are allusions to the Savior who would rescue the people from their sin. In order for us to recognize Him when He comes on the scene in the New Testament, His birthplace is identified, His mission is described, and the suffering and death He would endure as part of the rescue is forecasted. When He appears in the New Testament, everything transpires exactly as written about thousands of years earlier. The Hero, the Savior, was always there in the story even though history had not yet happened. The story of Jesus, born of a virgin in a little town called Bethlehem, was referenced in the Old Testament before history records that He was born of a virgin in a little town called Bethlehem.

Some ask: Could someone have constructed the ending after the fact to fit with the beginning? Really? Could Jesus have planned in utero His birth of a virgin, in the town of Bethlehem? Could He have orchestrated illegal tribunals that would convict Him? Could He have planned His persecution, the piercing of His side, a crown of thorns placed on His head? Could He have put together all the chain of events that led to His death on the cross? There are many prophecies in the Old Testament. Could one man construct his life to fulfill them all?

The unified nature of the story also argues for its authenticity as divinely inspired and written. No mere man or woman could put a book together as the Bible was and tell one seamless story. Consider these facts: 1. The Bible is composed of sixty-six books. Unlike other writings, it wasn't written in one person's lifetime, but rather, it was recorded over thousands of years, by many different individuals. 2. The Old Testament comprises thirty-nine books and describes events spanning thousands of years. 3. The human authors who recorded the individual books didn't themselves live in the same generation. 4. The New Testament history begins four hundred years after the last event recorded in the Old Testament. Therefore, the writers of the Old Testament had no way of knowing how the history would proceed beyond their deaths, and yet all transpires as they had written.

The entire story was planned from the beginning and only God could have written it. He is in control. By writing HIStory as He did, God demonstrated just how great His love for us is.

"For God so loved the world, that he gave His only Son, that whoever believes in him should not perish but have eternal life."

- J O H N 3 : 1 6

APPENDIX

Appendix

The order of the books of the Bible in the chart below are primarily chronological

THE OLD TESTAMENT	
Genesis	In the beginning God created...
	Man/Woman sinned
	God promised Abraham 1) numerous descendants 2) the Promised land 3) blessing to the nations through his descendant
	A sacrifice of an innocent would atone for sins.
	Cycle began: Sin of man/Judgment / Hope given
Exodus	Picture of Redemption and deliverance: God rescued Israel from slavery in Egypt/ He raised up Moses
	God gave Israel the Law
Leviticus	A call to worship God/ The high priest would intercede for the people.
Numbers	The people grumbled/ God ordained 40 years of wandering before they would enter the Promised Land with a new generation.
Deuteronomy	Moses' Farewell Speech: He encouraged Israel to Obey God, and God alone
Joshua	Joshua led the people into the Promised Land/ the land was portioned to the 12 tribes of Israel
Judges	God established a theocracy. He would be King, but gave Judges
Ruth	Story of life under the Judges/Picture of redemption
1st & 2nd Samuel	Record of Samuel who anointed the first kings of Israel
	Establishment of David's reign
	Promise of God expanded: "When your days are over and you rest with your fathers, I will raise up your offspring to succeed you, who will come from your own body, and I will establish his kingdom"
Psalms	Book of poetry regarding the attributes of God

1st & 2nd Kings	Record of the kings
	The Divided Kingdom established/ Israel to the north and Judah to the south
1st & 2nd Chronicles	Genealogies recorded /parallel account of the Kings
Job	God's power over Satan demonstrated
	Word of future redemption given: "I know that my redeemer lives, and that in the end he will stand on the earth. And after my skin has been destroyed, yet in my flesh I will see God." Job 19:25-26.
Proverbs	Book of wisdom
Ecclesiastes	Cynical account of life written by Solomon
Song of Solomon	Book of love/ Marriage is a gift of God and picture of God's relationship with His people.
Prophets to the Northern Kingdom/ Israel	Message: Warnings of Judgment
	prepare to meet your God
Amos	Picture of forgiveness for unfaithfulness
Hosea	
Prophets to the Nations:	"Message: Warnings to the enemies of Israel
	Warning to Edom
Obadiah	Prophet to Nineveh
Jonah	Warning of destruction to Nineveh
Nahum	

Appendix

Prophets to the Southern Kingdom/ Judah	"Message: Warnings of Judgment
	Locust invasion is a forecast of future judgment
Joel	Picture of Future Redeemer: His birth and ministry
Isaiah	Warning of Babylonian captivity
Micah	Lament over nation's sinfulness
Zephaniah	
Jeremiah (and his book of Lamentations)	
Habakkuk	
Prophets to the Kingdom while in Captivity	Message: Promises of Hope
	Promise of Protection/ Forecast of the Messianic Kingdom
Daniel	
Ezekiel	
Esther	Picture of God's protection of His people in order to preserve the Promise
Prophets after the release from Captivity/ Return to the Promised Land	Message: Rebuild the temple
	Priest who led first group back to Promised land
	Governor who led 2nd group
Ezra	Message: Rebuild the temple
Nehemiah	A future king promised
Haggai	
Zechariah	The last prophet/ A promise of one to come who would prepare the way for the Redeemer"
Malachi	
THE NEW TESTAMENT	The Savior comes/ the Story continues with us

Matthew	"Promises fulfilled... The Savior comes! Jesus is the Messiah"
Mark	Jesus is the Christ, the mighty worker
Luke	Jesus is the universal Savior
John	Jesus is the Son of God
Acts	The Holy Spirit at Work: History of the early Church Experiences of Peter and Paul/"Go & make disciples"
I Thessalonians	"Be joyful always; pray continually; give thanks in all circumstances, for this is God's will for you in Christ Jesus."
II Thessalonians	We must persevere in the faith
I Corinthians	We have a new life in Christ/ united in sound doctrine/ our body is the temple of the Holy Spirit
II Corinthians	We are being transformed into His likeness
Ephesians	We are created to do good works but we are saved by grace alone
Philippians	We have joy in Christ and are to have a generous heart
Colossians	We should make Christ our Lord of all
Galatians	We have freedom in Christ
Romans	We are saved by grace
Philemon	We have brotherhood/sisterhood in Christ
I Timothy	We need to oppose false doctrine and "fight the good fight of faith."
II Timothy	We need to keep sound doctrine
Titus	We need to stand firm in the gospel of grace
James	We are given a practical letter of Kingdom living
I Peter	We should expect suffering and persecution

II Peter	We need to continue in Godly living
I John	We have Christ who will forgive our sins
II & III John	We need to beware of false doctrine
Jude	We must contend for the faith
Hebrews	We have Christ, the better sacrifice
Revelation	Eternal Hope: Evil will be destroyed. Promise of a new heaven and new earth

Made in the USA
Middletown, DE
11 October 2021